YOU DON'T
TO KNOW HOW TO
MEDITATE

WHY IT'S WORTH NOT
KNOWING ANYTHING

by

MAXIMUS WALSH

This is dedicated to you.
To those of you I have already met, thank you,
for teaching me so much.
If I am yet to meet you, thank you,
for what you will teach me.

CONTENTS

YOU DON'T WANT TO KNOW HOW TO MEDITATE

ALL YOU CAN DO IS FIGURE IT OUT AS YOU GO ALONG

The choice to sit down and "do nothing" turns out to be harder than most would imagine. There is always so many other things that we would rather be doing, and with a world offering us so much, why would we want to sit and "do nothing" at all? Fortunately, it is quite impossible to **literally** do nothing, for there is always something happening; we have just become used to not paying it any attention. Meditation allows us to tune in to what is happening in this present moment and discover there is plenty enough going on for us to focus our attention on.

We are born into this life, and rarely do we stop for a moment and give some thought to what this whole "life" business even is. Like a wind-up toy you would find in a Christmas cracker, as soon as we have exploded onto the scene, we get going. We spend the beginning portion of this experience figuring out how to use some strange vehicle that we refer to as a body, exploring what each sensation means to us and those around us, and then before we realise it, we are so wrapped up in our lives that we get swept away with all of its goings on until the years pass, and we look back wondering where it all went. Like a wind-up toy, we need a lot of attention initially to ensure we don't head right off the edge of the table, but we can only be looked after for so long before we have to navigate ourselves along the path and through the obstacles that life may present us. What if you are headed for a fall and you don't see it? What if there is a dead end ahead? Maybe you're already at this end, and no matter how hard you keep trying to push on, you aren't getting anywhere. One thing we may not have had the option to learn was how to stop and be in stillness. A skill that allows us to see that we have the time to walk a path that we choose with every step.

Learning to meditate gives us the ability to slow down, take a moment and choose the next step. It gives us the time to see our options. Life is a hike in the woods, not a sprint on the racetrack. We need to pace ourselves and set out a clear route through the unknown, to see the checkpoints ahead and give us a clear direction to aim for. Consistency and a relaxed discipline will always lead to outcome, whether it is the outcome that you aimed for or not, there will always be a care package waiting ahead. Your persistence will always prove fruitful.

What can meditation do for you? Honestly, meditation can do whatever you want it to. More peace? Better sleep? Less frustration? Whatever you think of, meditation will aid you in your pursuit. Sounds a bit implausible, I know, but hear me out. Can you do anything without your mind? There may be "mindless" activities in our lives, but whatever we do, our mind is always involved. Meditation guides us towards discovering our minds, to be aware of what is going on inside of it and choose how we use the information we find passing through. Our practice allows us to create space between us and our thoughts, and the ability to let go of the ones that no longer benefit us.

We like to think we know our minds; it is ours after all. Yet, to know something is not to understand it. To know something is like having all the answers to the theory of a driving exam but never having sat in the driver's seat, whereas to understand is to have the ability to do a handbrake turn straight into your garage. Can you say that everything you think about is to your benefit? Do you always speak kindly to yourself and to others? Can you say you have never looked back on a choice or an action that you took and in hindsight realised there was a better way of handling that situation? There will always be moments where we slipped up from being the best versions of ourselves, but accepting we are not perfect all the time is an important pill to swallow, one that may have even been the reason you decided to learn how to meditate? The foolish think themselves to be the wise, but the wisest know themselves to be the fool.

You can read all the essays, books, and articles in the world on meditation, but until you sit down and practice, you will never be able to truly understand. Not everything is to be known. We can know many things and spout off many bits of information, but this is simply the regurgitation of information and all it really indicates is a great ability to remember. Much like the smelling of a rose, meditation cannot be known; you can only experience it.

I have written this book to share what I have come to understand over the years of training and practicing, to offer to you the exercises that led me to insights that enabled me to direct my life toward a life where I was in the driver's seat.

COMMON MISCONCEPTIONS

"I don't think I can meditate"

Were you able to read the first time you picked up a book? Were you able to spell your name the first time you picked up a pen? Reading and writing is a skill, just like meditation. There may be those fortunate few who manage to be more inclined to the ability than others, but even for them, there will still be forms of meditation that requires practice before it is perfected and understood. There was a time you could not do half of the things that you do now, yet now you can, and they require no effort as that skill has become natural to you. So it is with meditation. In time, with a regular commitment and practice, it will be as effortless as reading these words.

"Meditation is sitting and doing nothing"

When you sit and meditate, on the outside it may seem as though you are doing nothing, but the act of drawing our focus inward allows us to become aware that there is much happening, more than we can be fully aware of at the same time. Every part of you is having its own experience, different physical sensations can be found all over the body, and the body is only the top layer of our experience. When you start to delve deeper inside, then you realise it's not only ogres that are like onions. Even when you think you have managed to peel back the last layer, there is always another. One thing you will never be able to do is nothing.

"I am not able to sit for that long"

It does not matter the length of time that you can sit and meditate. To have the tendency to time our meditations only leads to competition; competing against ourselves and against others. This also leads us to think that the point of meditation is to get it done. The point of meditation is to simply be. The perception of time, especially as a mode of measurement, is a constraint to the freedom of the Self. You cannot find stillness of the mind in the constant counting of life.

You cannot be told how to meditate.

Language is incapable of explaining many things, and one of those things is meditation. If I sit here and try to write out my experience with meditation, then you will go in search of that same experience. Rather than chasing the counting of time, you will be chasing the meaning of words. What if you interpret my words differently than I had intended? What if my perception of happiness or sadness or stillness is different to yours? You will be sitting meditating, every time waiting for that thing you read about once, and it will never come; you will start to think that you cannot meditate. A carrot on a string will lead you in circles, as we are not looking for something ahead of us but looking at the experience we are having in the immediate present. Meditation is a lot like sleeping, I can tell you all the tips and techniques to help you prepare to go to sleep, but the actual falling asleep part is up to you. With meditation, I can tell you all the tips and techniques to get prepared to meditate, but the actual meditation part is something only you can manage to find yourself in.

You will not always be comfortable. It is not going to be easy.

As you use your body and mind in ways like never before, discomfort will arise. I warn all who do my meditation course that this path is not always a walk in the park. Every course or retreat that I have attended for meditative practices has always had a percentage of people drop out, those that choose to walk away rather than see it to the end. I have been close to throwing in the towel many times. Even lying flat on your back on the floor can be a struggle for some initially. Do not allow this to dissuade you from persisting, it is a part of the process. It is natural to seek a passive life - our first 9 months before we were even born, we had everything we needed. Yet we decide eventually that it is time to join the world. For a time, we must have everything done for us, until one day we become aware of what we are capable of, and off we go, encountering new challenges and directions of growth. You have already done it so many times before - This is a comforting idea when it is time to do it again.

You are not aiming to control your mind.

Rather, we are teaching ourselves to work **with** it. To control something is to restrict it, to have it conform to a way in which we want it to, which means suppression of how it is. Suppression of this kind leads to the destruction of the expression, and we must always express ourselves to live in honesty. Working with our mind rather than controlling it is like learning to dance with our partner. Rather than forcing a pace that leads to you both falling over each other's feet, you need to figure out what style you can both dance to.

When beginning your meditation practice, as you look to focus your concentration you may find the slightest of external disturbances will distract you. In terms of evolution, this distractedness as part of our fight or flight instinct has been a necessary requirement to survival and without it, it is unlikely we would have made it this far. Take humankind back a few millennia, if you were foraging in the bushes and you hear a movement rustling where you cannot see, you need to react without wasting time to think if the sound is a threat to life or not. In those lives, the environment was a dangerous place, full of unknowns that could not be predicted or controlled, but over the generations of many, we have shaped our environment to be almost devoid of any threat at all. Yet the mechanism remains. We have made our outer world safe, and now is the time to secure the inner world. This archaic programme that is a part of our operating system is still looking out for threats to be wary of, and rather than just identifying the dangers to our lives, it now recognises dangers to who we believe we are. It is our attachment to the idea of our self that confuses our nervous system into perceiving psychological threat as a genuine life threat.

1 Learn how to actually relax.

▨ TIME TO CHILL.

Think of a time you have lain on the floor, flat on your back, belly to the sky. Probably haven't, right? If you have, raise your hand. Put your hand down if you have done this for more than 20 minutes. Put your hand down if you have done this for more than 45 minutes. Hands down for more than 60. Are there any hands left up? The only time we ever allow ourselves to lay down is on a bed or a sofa, often not flat on our backs, but numerous other body shapes, with pillows and cushions etc, making us less like a straight line and more like a squiggly wiggle.

Lying flat on your back is the only way that your spine is totally supported, and your body can completely relax. Your spine is the house to the central nervous system, the main hub of all you are, with the brain stuck to the top. If your brain was a computer screen, then your central nervous system is your computer's remaining hardware. The energy for the function of all we do passes through this central hub, and so any misalignment in the spine causes kinks and pressures on the pathways of the energy moving through you. Any pressure or tension on the spine, on all that we are, causes an alertness and reactive state in the body keeping us awake and the body never fully drops into a true relaxation and repair state.

Your central nervous system comprises of 2 energies, your sympathetic nervous system, and your parasympathetic nervous system. The sympathetic part is the conscious, decision energy, the part that works with you to move your body and consists of what you choose to do. The parasympathetic regions are to do with your unconscious goings on, such as the functioning of your organs and the repairing of your body. There are areas where these 2 energies overlap such as your blinking or breathing, however we can only interrupt these for a short period of time before the necessity of the functioning of this parasympathetic behaviour overpowers our conscious action.

Our first practice is a relaxation. This exercise works with the parasympathetic areas of the spine, as when we lay on our backs, the sympathetic area is not engaged – therefore we can sleep better laying down instead of sitting up.

To lay on the ground, set yourself down a blanket or a mat and then lay flat on your back with space between your

*legs and your armpits. In a yoga asana (posture) practice
this pose would be called Savasana (corpse pose). Have
the palms of your hands facing the sky and stretch out
your legs with your feet flopped to the sides. Bring your
shoulder blades in toward each other, then try to press
each part of your spine into the floor, your lower back, and
the back of your neck, so now your chin tucks in slightly
as you lengthen through the whole of your spine. Then let
go. Allow your body to be however it wants and relax. (If
you have any complaints in your lower back, bend your
knees and place your feet on the floor, wider than hip
width apart with the knees resting against each other so
that you do not need to hold them there.)*

*As you lay here in Savasana, close your eyes, and bring
your attention to your breath. Be aware of every sensation
your breath brings along with it. The cool air coming in
through the nostrils. The warmer breath passing back out.
The expansion and contraction of your rib cage, of your
whole body. Be present in the feeling. Then, once you have
settled, bring your attention to your right foot. As you take
a deep breath in, contract and squeeze all the muscles in
your right foot. Curl your toes in, squeeze the muscles to
the bone and press it down into the floor. As you exhale,
release. Allow your right foot to rest however it may fall.
Take a moment, then bring your awareness up your right
leg into the lower leg, connecting to your calf muscles,*

your shin, and repeat the practice with the breath here. Inhale to squeeze and contract, exhale to release and let go. Continue this practice with the whole of your body, part by part, piece by piece. Go through your body and use every muscle, as strong and as hard as you can. Follow any route that works naturally for you. Travel your body and explore every area of it.

Don't forget your pelvic floor muscles, pulling them up inside / each butt cheek, and then both / your abdominals, pushing your belly button away from you. Then again, now pulling your belly button into your spine / Squeezing your chest, pulling your pectorals into you / with your shoulder blades, squeezing them back in toward your spine / pull your shoulders up to your neck / lift your head high off the floor to work your neck. Push your head back on to the floor as strong as you can / open your mouth wide, let your jaw loosen / Stick your tongue out as far as you can / Scrunch your face in as small as possible / Squeeze your eyes closed tightly into their sockets / Raise your eyebrows as high as you can / Anywhere and everywhere else!

Once you have tensed and released every muscle in your body, rest your attention on the crown of your head. Whether you feel anything or not, just be aware this part of you exists. Finally, with one more deep breath in, squeeze/contract/press/tense every single part of your body, tighter, tighter, tighter, until with a long exhale you totally release everything and your whole body can soften and relax.

Rest. Be in the stillness. Every part of your body has had attention, every muscle has now released and relaxed, so stay here a while and give your body the chance to fully rest. But remain focused. As you find stillness in your body, continue to move your focus of attention around each part of your body as if you were still tensing it with every inhale. Be present in every sensation and feeling as you continue to explore yourself. Stay here for as long as you can afford. Give yourself this time that you may never have done before. If you end up falling asleep, excellent! If you fall asleep then it is because that is what your body needed.

Something you may experience at some point in this relaxation is, as you lay on the floor for a while, suddenly you may find yourself twitch or spasm. The intensity can range from quite small, to a whole limb flinging itself randomly. Do not be alarmed at this, it is quite natural and simply a releasing of tension. This practice is all about releasing and letting go, requiring very little from you except to allow whatever comes to happen without interruption. There is no "what should be happening", nothing to look for, just a resting in awareness of what is.

For some of us, this practice can present discomfort in many forms. Aching or emotions may present themselves. This is good. Allow them to be there. Aim not to dismiss them, to not label them as undesirable or "bad" as may be the initial reaction. To interrupt the process will not take you away from this discomfort, it will only serve as a distraction; what you wish to get away from is yourself. We cannot escape these things, we either let them go or carry them with us wherever we go. Observe these experiences in the same way as any other sensation in your body. Guide your focus over these things, without thinking on them. If you cannot, do not worry, this will become easier as you practice and settle deeper into the space between you and your thoughts.

As you treat your body to better rest, in time you will be less likely to fall asleep during this relaxation and so you may find that as you practice this in future, you remain awake and aware for longer. The longer you practice, the more likely your mind is to wander, so as much as possible remember to catch yourself and come back to resting your focus inside the body. Whatever the case may be, never think on what you 'should' or 'could' be doing, do not have an aim with your practice, just allow whatever happens to happen. Give up control.

2 Harness your concentration.

▓ LET'S GET FOCUSED.

Your focus is omnipresent, observing you through the day and night, watching your waking life, watching your dreams; it never sleeps. We can direct/harness this focus, deciding what we guide it toward as each unique experience unfolds around us. But like any tool, if we do not maintain and take care of our focus then it can become less effective and harder to use. Do you ever find yourself becoming distracted? That your focus seems to be drift to something other than what you are doing now?

How often are you fully concentrated on the task at hand? Your body may be in the shower, but your mind is in the conversation you had with your partner earlier. Your body may be eating or drinking but your mind is considering if you want to commit to that thing you said you would do this weekend. Harnessing your concentration is a full-time practice, always checking in with whatever you are doing, that all your attention is to your immediate experience. There is always time to think on things, but make sure that you are thinking on the things that you wish to think on. I have been asked in the past whether spacing out and the mind w(o/a)ndering is meditation, but this is absent-mindism which is, if anything, the complete opposite of what we aim to achieve in our practice. In these moments, our mind has taken over completely and is lost in whatever it is thinking about...until you snap back, and you cannot remember what it was you were thinking about to begin with. To be present is to be aware of where we are, both physically and mentally. How often are you thinking of things that end up hurting you? If we are not fully paying attention then a train of thought can suddenly come hurtling through the station, taking you away with it.

Think of your friend who is the longest possible drive from you. You plot the route and aim for the quickest option available. We may set off with the intention of travelling from A to B, but not every task is so easy to complete. Sometimes it's like we want to go to that friend's house but stop by every other friend along the way. Some may think "well no, it would be more the fact that every road is a dead end or diverted traffic" and although on occasion this may seem true, the ultimate truth is that you are choosing to get distracted and allowing your mind to w(a/o)nder. Getting to your furthest friend is an impossible task for one day and so you go back home. Giving up is just that easy.

Have you ever thought on what concentration is? The idea of concentrating is as if it were a constant fixation of attention, like the light of a bulb shining down on the object of focus. It is also seen as something to be used, and then used up, as if concentration were like a battery, a small reserve of energy. If this were true, then how have you made it to this word you are reading this very moment? If concentration were the fixation of attention, you would never have made it past the first word, or even the first letter! Concentration is the constant refocusing of your attention, such as reading the letters of a word, and the words of this sentence.

Anapana is a powerful tool in building the strength of your focus, and a simple practice to build the foundation of your discipline on. To perform Anapana, all you need to do is watch your breath. Close your eyes and be aware of the sensation of your breathing in your nose. Only in your nose. Fully focus on the sensation that is most prevalent. Maybe it's around the nostrils, the cool air coming with the inhale, or the warmer breath coming back out. (At which point does air become breath? Or breath become air?)

As you sit, eventually your attention may distract itself to other things. Ok, no problem. There is no need to get hung up on this, it is the nature of your mind and you can only work with how it is, not how you wish it were. The distraction is not a failing of the practice, the distractions will always present themselves, you simply need to notice you have become distracted. Whenever you manage to catch yourself and notice that your attention has left the breath for other things, bring it back. Catch yourself and bring your focus back to your breathing. Each time you do this is like a bicep curl at the gym, with each repetition you increase the strength of your focus 'muscles'. Catching your awareness and returning it to the breath is not starting over, it is a part of the process and a part of your progress. Repeat. Repeat. Repeat.

Give yourself whatever time you can afford, and then, when you have finished, let go of the practice. It does not matter how well you think you did, whether you caught your mind once or twenty times, let it go and move on with the rest of your day. Sometimes you sit for a while and catch yourself many times, other times you sit and can't seem to catch yourself at all. That is how it is. Do not compare this sitting with your last sit, all that matters is that you gave yourself the time to practice. Each practice is progress, whether it feels like it or not.

Another technique to help you work on your concentration is the practice of Trataka. Trataka involves sitting and staring at an object, closing your eyes, and then holding the image in your mind's eye until it fades, and then repeating.

The object can be anything, although it is better to use something alive and beautiful, such as a flower. This is an excellent way to understand how to bring your focus from the outside to the inside.

One of the better items to begin with is a lit candle. Light a candle and place it at eye level, allowing you to remain tall with a long spine rather than looking down and having your head tilted forwards. Softly gaze at the flame of the candle, you do not need to 'concentrate hard', your face should be relaxed. Soften your eyebrows, soften your jaw. Fix your eyes on the top of the wick in the flame so your eyes can remain on a fixed point rather than following the movement of the flame itself. Watch the flame long enough until you feel that the image is well burned into your vision, and then close your eyes. You can still 'see' the flame. Focus on this residual image, in whatever form it may present itself, whether it is just as you saw it, a different part of the candle or the colours are inverted, it does not matter. Whatever you see, hold that in your focus. Holding this in your vision, the stronger the force of your concentration, the longer the image shall remain. Eventually the image may fade, or your mind may w(a/o)nder, and when this happens all you need to do is repeat.

Another way to practice Trataka is to stare at the flame of the candle and not blink at all. Sit there, gazing at the flame and do not close your eyes. Your eyes will begin to water, but continue, the watering is keeping your eyes from drying out, so you can continue with your practice for longer. This technique will build a stronger connection to your eyes, allowing you to work them in a way as you may never have done before. Our eyes are muscles, and just like any other muscle, unless it is taken care of, it will start to weaken.

These 2 forms of practicing this Trataka technique can also be used together, beginning with the open-eyed staring for as long as you feel, until you close your eyes and continue the practice inside. Experiment! It is the key to finding your way into an effective meditation practice.

Before entering our meditations, we must first understand and integrate the idea of acceptance. Acceptance is a key element to the foundation of any successful practice. But what does it mean to accept something? It is not saying "this is ok" or ignoring whatever the experience may be. It is being aware but not engaged. You already have this ability. Consider for a moment whatever may be going on in your environment as you read this. Maybe there are other people to notice or sounds to hear, but until this moment you have kept your focus on reading. These things are a part of your environment and should you so choose, you can give them your attention. Yet, you have accepted your surroundings in order to remain engaged on the desired task, quite literally leaving them as background noise. If you were trying to ignore these things, then you would find that you are distracted and a part of your focus, if not all of it, is caught up in the distraction around you, but in denial. From an outside perspective your focus is on the task at hand, but internally you are working hard to deny the distraction any signs of attention.

Accepting your surroundings will be essential in your meditations, for the goings on around you are beyond your control. If you are sitting to practice and into your space comes an obnoxious foul-smelling individual, this intrusion will distract you, but what can you do about the actions of another? You could get up and move somewhere else, but what happens when there is nowhere left for you to move to? Embrace all that happens when you sit to meditate, accept the challenge offered to you and use it to strengthen your practice. What we consider to be distractions are our own attachments to ideas we never chose to think about. We will come to this at the end of the next chapter. For now, hold the idea of accepting all things:

- Your surroundings, the happenings around you.
- Your sensations, the experience of your senses of the outside and inside world.
- Yourself, the thoughts, and conjuring's of the mind that stir in the shallows all the way to the depths.

All that happens when we meditate is meant for our meditation, offering us the chance to learn something about who we are.

3 Welcome to the "Real".

▨ LET'S GET PHYSICAL.

How does it feel to be you? Not emotionally, we'll get to that, for now I mean physically. Raise your right hand and point your index finger. Give your right index finger your full attention. Can you feel it? The sensations of that finger on the surface of the skin? Now feel the finger from the inside. From the fingertip to the palm of your hand. What does it feel like? Spread this awareness to other fingers, then to your hand...Can you feel the whole of you? If you touch every part of your body, can you feel that sensation? Maybe, here a bit more, there a bit less... Some areas of your body feel sensitive, other areas less so. How about without stimulus? Without a loud and immediate sensation, our body can seem dull. It requires input to bring our awareness to the quieter parts of ourselves. Imagine yourself as a colour by numbers, little sections collated together to form your whole physical body. Every day you wake up, you colour in a few of these sections, the areas you give the most attention to. Every night the colours fade from out of these sections. Over time, the parts that you colour in the most have a build-up of colour and are the most vivid of your creation, yet the parts of you that you pay the least attention to require a lot more colouring before they match the rest of your artwork. The levels of colour around your body is the strength of your self-awareness, of your connection to your form. Physical awareness will be different from person to person - it depends on how you have used your body most of your life. Focus on the most sensitive area of your body, not in terms of pain but height of awareness, the part of your body that you are most in tune with. Compare that to the part of your body you feel to be the least sensitive. Why is there such a difference? It all depends on the connection between body and minds (for we have more than one...more about that when we come to Chakras.)

Have you ever thought about how you sit? Most of us know that we should be "sitting up straight" but has anyone ever told you how? Our spines may seem like they are meant to be a straight line from top to bottom, and from the back or front it would look somewhat straight, but when you visualise your spine you need to see it from the side. The best way to set your spine is to make sure it has a smooth S curve from top to bottom. Begin with the base of your spine, your tailbone tucked between your hips. When sitting, tilt the pelvis forward, like you're trying to sit more on your genitals than your bum. In doing this, the base of your spine is now positioned near enough perfectly for you to sit with a well-supported spine. As you tilted your pelvis, you may have noticed your spine lengthening upwards and your chest opening. Add a little extra to the opening of your chest by bringing your shoulder blades back and down behind you. Not too much, we are not trying to puff ourselves up like a pigeon, so don't have your ribs sticking out in front of you, just providing ourselves a little more opening and a bit more breathing space. Depending on how strong and/or flexible your core muscles may be will also play a role in how comfortably you can sit for a long period of time, but as with any new way of using your body, it will adapt.

One thing to note, if your knees are higher than your hips, the tilt in the pelvis will be hard to maintain. You want to be pouring your hips downhill, not uphill, so however or whatever way that you are sat, it is often the case that putting a few pillows under your bum or being sat on the edge of your seat will aid you. What you do with your legs is unimportant. There are many different ways of sitting, each with their own benefits and drawbacks, whether you are sat on the floor, a pillow, a chair, or with your legs wrapped up like a pretzel, it is a matter of capabilities when it comes to being sat as to what you choose to do with your legs. The important point to focus on is the setting of your spine.

Checking in on your posture is a good way to check in with yourself and to make sure you are still fully engaged. Our posture is a loud reflection of our minds. Body language is a huge part of communication with others, it is a language you are already fluent in, so we can use this to listen to ourselves. If you start to drop your chin, or your spine starts to lean forward or to the side, then this is a sign of fatigue and/or loss of focus. If you start lifting your chin higher, you are trying too hard or have got carried away in a train of thought. Any expression on your face such as a furrowed brow, or even if your eye lids are fluttering, is an indication that you are thinking about something. Be soft.

One more tip for sitting is what to do with your tongue. Often, I see people sitting who end up with a mouth full of saliva who feel they shouldn't swallow for that would make too much noise and break the stillness of their practice. It's ok, you can swallow when needed! I used to be one of those people, sitting there with cheeks puffed out and my tongue floating around. However, I found the way to avoid this completely was to rest the tip of my tongue on the roof of my mouth just behind my teeth. This will prevent a build-up of saliva in the mouth and give you one less thing to be distracted by. I have practised this so much that my tongue now automatically rests here, as I have only just noticed whilst typing these very words. There is always something new to discover with yourself. (I have heard that our tongue rests at the bottom of our mouth if English is the language that we speak, and that those who have an eastern European dialect naturally have their tongue resting against the top of their mouth. If this is apocryphal or not, I am yet to discover.)

Seated, spine set, tongues at the ready! Now you are ready to practice a meditation. Our first meditation is basically the same practice as the relaxation we did before, tensing and relaxing areas of the body as we breathe, the only difference being that now you are sat up, so the sympathetic region of your spine is active. See how this changes your practice. To prepare, it is always a good habit to begin with some Anapana, taking a moment to get yourself centred and focused. Once you have settled, do the same practice as you did when you lay on the floor, taking your focus to parts of your body, tensing with the inhale, and relaxing with the exhale. Slowly and patiently, feeling each part of your anatomy, from the muscle down to the bone, move your awareness around your whole being until you find the top of your head where you hold your focus. After some time spent here, finish with a full body squeeze, clenching and tightening all of you with a deep breath until you exhale and fully release every part of your body. Now, sit in the stillness, body softly engaged to hold you upright. Focus on feeling. Be in your body. No thoughts need thinking about, stay engaged with what sensations are present in your experience. Stay engaged with the practice by continuing to take your awareness around your body, continuing to explore each part of your anatomy with the same level of focus as if you were still tensing with the inhale. Feel what sensations are present without the louder input.

You may find as you practice this exercise for longer periods of time that the experience in some form becomes undesirable. Feelings of discomfort, or emotions we would rather not feel begin to present themselves. This is where our practice of acceptance must come in to play.

So, you are aware of a sensation you do not like, something you wish to avoid. How does one react to this? We tend to move away from it, engaging ourselves in something else. But this feeling is not a result of the location you were just in. If you were to sit and do your practice somewhere else, a similar situation would develop. If you were to return to the space you were just sat, would the sensation return? This experience is nothing to do with the location, so we are not getting away from anything in avoidance, for the thing you are trying to avoid is in you. You are attached in aversion to it.

Aversion is one end of a spectrum, where craving is at the other. The spectrum of attachment. To crave something is to be addicted, to fear being without it. To have an aversion to something is to fear it, to wish it to never come into our lives at all. These attachments come from fear; the fear of not having enough or the fear of the thing itself. To be addicted to something is to be afraid of who you will be without what you are addicted to. What you are addicted to is a welcome distraction from reality. You may be addicted to the point that you do not know who you are, were you to be without it. To live in total avoidance of something is to have a phobia, to try to live in a reality where something does not exist, even though it does. But to live in denial does not make it true. You may believe it to be a threat or danger to you, or it may make you see something that is an uncomfortable truth you wish to believe does not exist, forcing you to live in ignorance. It is not the items of our attachments we must seek to be free from, but the fear that is held to it.

Our attachments can come in many forms and for many reasons. But it is a spectrum, as shown here:

Aversion< - - - Hate - - - < - - - Dislike - - - < 0 > - - - Like - - - > - - - Love - - - > Craving

As with all spectrums, there are many differing degrees in either direction, and as we go through life, encountering new experiences, we categorise each event or item somewhere along this spectrum, sometimes consciously but often unconsciously. We remember this information for future use, so that we may indulge in more of the things that we prefer. I am sure for many of us, there will have been a vegetable we hated as a child. Whenever we found it on our plate we would groan and complain of our disgust by it. That disgust may have continued for a long time, until much later in our lives when that same disgust would be there, even though you have not tried it now for many years. Then for some reason, someday, maybe you decide you will try it, and even as you take the first bite that disgust is still there until you notice that actually...it's quite nice! (I used to have this with fish...used to hate the stuff, but now I can't get enough.) Without being aware of this way of functioning within ourselves, we will go through our whole lives in avoidance of experiences that may be to our pleasure or our benefit.

Avoidance will be the primary feeling you regularly encounter in a meditation practice, there is not much to get addicted to (though a spiritual addiction is a potential trap we can fall into.) What we are looking to achieve within our practice is to centre ourselves in that < 0 > point of the spectrum, that point where we are on neither side of the fence but perfectly balanced between either end. A place of total acceptance, in the state of an equanimous mind. Within this place of balance, you can witness your experience without attachment, no longer categorising and labelling anything but seeing it as it is. Eventually you step outside of the spectrum entirely and find yourself experiencing life from a different perspective – you now have the tool of a "birds eye view."

We subscribe ourselves to many mindset modalities, all of which are spectrums we use to measure our experiences. Whether it's being nasty or nice, good or bad, optimistic or pessimistic, etc. To live our lives by these ideals will always have you subjected to its fluctuating options; you cannot have heaven without hell. To be in joy will always be measured against sorrow. It is like standing on a train track with the knowledge of an oncoming train. Some will choose to watch the approaching train, focusing on the negative end of the spectrum. Others will choose to face the other direction and, with the knowing of the train in the back of their minds, enjoy the scenery of distant mountains until that final moment. In our practice, we suddenly find that we can step off the tracks. We no longer need to look one way or the other. We no longer need to measure the good by the bad, concepts that only exist in the thinking mind. When we are not busy thinking, then our intuition can be heard, and we can listen more clearly to its guidance.

Easier said than done; at least to begin with. When you are sat meditating and discomfort grows louder and louder, looking for a quiet mind will be challenging. When you can't concentrate on your practice any longer due to that pain in your back or that numbness in your foot, a perfectly balanced mind may be nowhere to be found. This is when we must remember the true nature of all phenomena in the universe. Impermanence (Anicca). Nothing is forever. All moments in life wash over us like waves from the ocean. Every feeling, every sensation, every sound, comes and goes. Every experience you have ever had, and will ever have, will be a moment lost in time. By now, you will have experienced a wide range of emotions, but you do not still feel them at this moment in time. The phenomena in our lives are as momentary as our concentration, requiring a constant refocusing of our awareness. We forget this when we are deep in despair or suffering, it seems to last for so long that it can feel like it is all there is and ever will be, but eventually it ends, and we continue through life as all humans do, as our ancestors did. Remember this when you are struggling in your discomfort. See if you can find out what happens when you do not scratch an itch. One of the best teachers you could ever have when you are trying to sit and observe your sensations without attachment is a mosquito.

However, should you end up at a point where the discomfort and pain you are experiencing is like a black hole to your awareness, sucking in your focus to a point that you cannot break free from, take a break. Slowly and patiently, close your practice, coming out of it in a calm and mindful way. Make it a conscious choice rather than a reactive one. This work can be achieved gradually, over many sittings. Do what you can each time you practice, you can always continue the work next time. Remember, the flower does not bloom in one day. It is a journey, not a sprint.

4 Your Energy, You're Energy.

■ LET'S GET ELECTRIC.

Within yoga there is a focus on the practice of Pranayama, which translates to "suspension of life force" that consist of various breathing practices, each designed for its own purpose. Prana = Life force, and Yama = extend/restrain/control. Take a moment before reading this chapter to practice a breathing technique known as Sama Vritti Pranayama, equal ratio breathing (translates as same/equal fluctuations).

Much like your Anapana practice, Sama Vritti requires you to observe your breathing but adds taking control of the breath and counting it. Deepen your breathing and notice that every breath is made of 4 parts; you have the inhale, and then a momentary internal retention of the breath, and then the exhale, with a momentary external retention of the breath. Breathing deeper, have each part of your breath be as long as the other, breathing in for a count of

4, holding for 4, exhaling for 4, and holding the exhale for a count of 4. The pace of the counting is whatever you find to be comfortable. You can count at a speed that you choose, maybe using the seconds on a clock or, if you can tune in, then using the beating of your heart/pulse as the measure to go by. Perform this practice for as long as you like, until you find yourself in a calm, centred and focused state. Nice.

We are in our own invisible ocean. It flows through us, around us and between us. Us and all things. It is electricity - we run on it! The primary source of energy that we consume is electricity. It has long been known in eastern traditions that there is an energy force that we need, and which we can harness. You may have heard of Prana or Chi. These terms are probably the most heard of, though I am sure there are many more, but from here on I shall refer to our electric energy as Prana, which translates from Sanskrit as "life force". It is this life force that brings our minds and bodies together, much in the same way a computer runs. Information is carried by electricity and the data is then transformed into mechanics and action, and vice versa, in a complete circuit. You click and drag the mouse on a computer screen, you click and press your finger from your consciousness. Breath is the bridge between the mind and the body.

The Prana you need is in the air around you, tiny little charged particles called "negative ions" and "positive ions". *** *Quick and basic science class here. Not essential, but interesting...* ***

Despite the name, it is the negative ions that provide us with the extra charge, though that does not mean that the positive ions do not also provide energy. In fact, the positive ions are the negatively charged particles. Both are a form of energy, and both provide us with what we need. Where the negative ions are the provider of a charged current, the positive ions provide a negative current, so a (+1) for the former and then a (−1) for the latter. However, do not see these energies as opposing, but complementary, like the left wing of a bird needs the right wing. ***Quick and basic science class ends!*** I am no electrician, and this is no science lesson, so there is no need to talk about electrons and protons or anions and cations, so leaving behind the language of science we will adopt the negative ion as Yang, and the positive ion as Yin.

Our Yang energy is our 'doing' energy. It is the direction and focus, connected to our sympathetic nervous system. Yin energy keeps everything running without our needing to focus on it. This includes the functioning of our organs and repairing of our bodies, connected to our parasympathetic nervous system. The symbol of a snake is often used to depict this idea, with the head of the snake being Yang and the body of the snake being Yin. One is not more essential than the other, they are both required and cannot exist alone, so it is possible that either may be an untapped source of power for the individual. Yin is the power, Yang is the direction, and when aligned, together they create a powerful force.

Visualise your spine as a snake, with its long and large body coiled, sitting, as the lower part of your spine, reaching all the way up to your brain which is the head of the snake. See it alert and watching, fangs exposed, and eyes fixed ahead, looking out from the centre of your forehead. Fully aware, totally engaged.

If you were to sprint as fast as you could for 100 metres, what is the first thing you do to restore your energy? You breathe! But are you breathing properly? Become aware of your breathing, and how your body performs this action. Where are you breathing from? Your nose or your mouth? Where are you breathing into? Are you breathing into your full lung capacity, or just the top of the lungs? Are you breathing into your belly - is your diaphragm moving? Most of us will go through our lives without ever considering the way that we breathe. If you are breathing shallow breaths, only breathing into the top of your lungs, chances are you are breathing through your mouth. If you are a mouth breather, you will be in a highly reactive state and the body will be constantly exposed to stress, and chances are that you often catch colds and bugs. There is no filter when we breathe through the mouth, whatever we inhale can lodge itself happily in the moist warm environment of our throats. Our nose comes with a filter. The mouth does not. It is a backup option if the nose is not available. The most efficient way for our body to breathe is in through the nose and from the belly so our diaphragm can help pump the lungs, pulling more breath in and squeezing more back out. With deep diaphragmatic belly breaths, we can use our maximum lung capacity. Deeper breathing = more oxygen + more prana.

This is the first step in learning how to become conscious of the unconscious, using our yang to reprogram our yin modalities. The way that we breathe is a habit, a programme, that has been created through our lives, but it is common for this programme to end up running inefficiently if we have not taken time to give it a tune up. We could be breathing through our mouths, breathing shallow breaths or it is even possible to squeeze the belly in when inhaling, which neutralises our diaphragm. Each habit will have its own resistance to being reprogrammed, but all can be corrected through regular conscious practice.

We utilise Yang and Yin energies most efficiently by breathing in through our nostrils. The energy comes in through the nose, travels through our body around a network of energetic channels/pathways known as Nadis, and then it passes out through our fingers and toes where we ground ourselves, discharging our bodies. (Wearing shoes all the time can interrupt this circulation of energy, so spend some time with your feet free, and practice walking on grass where possible.) Our left nostril is the Ida Nadi, responsible for our Yin energy being channelled into the body, with the right nostril being the Pingala Nadi, responsible for the Yang energy. One nostril tends to be dominant for around an hour a day before it switches to the other nostril as our body works to balance our

Prana. The dominant nostril can change at any point in the day, however, depending on what we get up to. For example, if we are exerting ourselves then it is likely that during that time our right nostril is dominant as that is the energy source we are using most rapidly, and then after we have exercised our left nostril will be dominant as the body seeks to rest and repair itself.

There is a practice called Nadi Shodhana Pranayama, alternate nostril breathing, (although it translates to "channel cleaning/purifying life force control") that seeks to bring Ida and Pingala Nadis into balance. Sit comfortably in a meditative position and settle here. Place your index finger and middle finger onto your forehead, with your thumb on one nostril and ring finger on the other. Closing one nostril, breathe in normally through the open one, then swap nostrils and breathe out through the other. Breathe in through that same, open nostril, and then swapping nostrils, breathe out through the other. Continue in this fashion, just passing your natural breath between the nostrils using your finger and thumb to open and close each one.

When you find you have connected to this practice, you can start taking deeper breaths, inhaling to your maximum lung capacity, and then exhaling, completely emptying your lungs. Other variations can bring a pause between the inhale and exhale, suspending the breath for a moment before the exhale, or if you prefer, you can add in your

Sama Vritti Pranayama, counting the breathing to have each part of the breath as long as the other.

Our Prana, as with all things, is constantly fluctuating. The energy we have available to us can change because of everything we do, both physically and mentally. We can also find ourselves with blockages in our systems, areas of our energy channels inside of us that create a path of resistance to the flow of our life force. These can manifest in many ways in the physical body, such as tension or "dead spots" where there is little connection or feeling, but although they are physical manifestations, the roots of them are energetic, metaphysical. Imagine your Nadis as a high-quality silver metallic wiring and at its first installation the wires are totally perfect and clean. Over time, as you go through life and encounter different stresses, they start to get bent and knotted with signs of wear and tear showing, and rust forming. These disruptions to the flow of energy in your body are dense, stagnant energies that reduce the natural flow of your life force passing through, like large stones in the riverbeds that cause sediment to build up as the river flows. With maintenance. the wires can be restored, the heavy energy can be moved on, and the flow of Prana through you can return to its optimum levels.

A powerful pranayama technique is a practice known as Tummo breathing, or as I like to call it, the "super Prana charger breath". With the practice of Tummo, we breathe in through the nose as deeply as we can , to our maximum lung capacity as quick as we can, and then exhale the breath out through the mouth, taking time at the end of the exhale to ensure we have completely emptied the lungs as we pull the belly in, pushing our diaphragms up to squeeze our lungs. We breathe in this way for a certain number of breaths, or for a period of time, and once completed, we sit our awareness in the space of our bodies to observe whatever has been moved inside of us. Initially practice something like 30 rounds of breath or breathing this way for a minute and see how you do. As you get more familiar with Tummo then you can start to increase how long each round is, attempting three rounds each time. Maintain the intensity of the practice throughout.

This breathing technique I call a super Prana charger pranayama as it powerfully circulates Prana around your body, pushing through any stagnant and dense energy that may be in there and recharges the body with a lot of new energy. To some of us, practicing this can feel uncomfortable as it can circulate suppressed emotional energy or we have become used to not having high levels of energy, and the difference this practice can create in us may seem intense, but do not be afraid of your own power. Ease yourself into the practice as you familiarise yourself with it, and gradually work harder as your confidence in it grows.

There is a third Nadi called the Sushumna (very gracious/kind) Nadi, and it is the channel that runs through the whole of your spine, from the base of it, up to the crown of the head - the snake. This Nadi threads through the spinal cord and all the major chakras (we will cover chakras in the next chapter), and when all energies are balanced and all energetic blockages have been cleared, our Kundalini energy travels through. Our Kundalini is a large reserve of energy that is imagined as a coiled snake, sleeping in our base chakra. Over time, through a regular practice, this snake begins to awaken, bringing a powerful yin energy threaded up through the Sushumna Nadi from the root chakra through all the major chakras and into the crown, bringing the unconscious to the conscious and bringing enlightenments to the practitioner.

It is important to be aware of this mechanism within your practice; we will talk more on this in the next chapter, but for now we will look to work with a practice that gives us a better understanding of the Sushumna Nadi and strengthens our connection with it. We have 3 energetic 'locks' in our body that can be used to catch circulating Prana and redirect the life force to an intended purpose. There is the root lock, the Mula Bandha, consisting of our pelvic floor muscles. To engage our root lock, we pull the pelvic floor muscles up into the body and hold. Initially, if you do not have a strong connection with your pelvic floor, then when you first begin to work this area of your body you will be engaging your genitals and anus. The pelvic floor we are aiming to engage is the muscles in between these two sets of muscles. The central lock, Uddiyana Bandha, uses our abdominals and core muscles of the gut, requiring the pulling in of the belly button to the spine and then trying to lift the belly button into the rib cage. Eventually you will be aiming to be able to pull back your gut to the point you can fit your fist where it normally would be. Finally, the throat lock, Jalandhara Bandha, which is a bit more mechanical than the other two locks in that to engage this lock one must bring their chin to their chest and then slide the head back, closing off the throat and opening the back of the neck, keeping the spine long; You will know when you have this correct as you will be able to hear your breath catching in your throat.

These locks should be worked individually so that you strengthen the connection to the muscles of these areas and work through any blockages or numb zones that may exist. The engagement of Mula Bandha catches the Prana that is travelling through you and then redirects your life force back up the Sushumna. After the root lock, we engage our central lock, Uddiyana Bandha, which acts as a pump or a bellows, squeezing our life force further up the spine toward our throat lock, which is where we catch the recirculated Prana, providing us with a current of Prana that now provides for our higher Chakras. Essentially, we catch in the root lock, push with the central lock, and hold with the throat lock.

To begin a practice with the locks of your body, finding a comfortable sitting position and with your eyes closed, start to take deep breaths. With every inhale, breathe deeper into your body until you can feel your breath travelling down into your pelvic floor muscles. Feel them expanding, and then with the exhale, pull the pelvic floor muscles into yourself for the duration of the out breath, engaging Mula Bandha. When you inhale again, maintain engagement with these muscles so you gently release them as you breathe back into your root. Continue the practice in this way so your pelvic floor moves with your breath the same way as your lungs do. As you strengthen your connection to this part of your body then you can start to introduce a pause in the practice at the deepest part of your exhale when the root lock is engaged at its strongest.

After some time working with Mula Bandha, bring your focus to the central lock and now work with this. As you inhale, the belly expands until you cannot breathe in any further, and then as you exhale, squeeze the belly button into the spine as you lift it up into your ribcage for the whole length of the exhale. With the next breath in, the belly expands again, and you continue to work with Uddiyana Bandha. As with Mula Bandha, when you have a stronger practice with this lock then you can look to work with a pause at the deepest part of the exhale when your central lock is fully engaged.

When you have given a lot of time and practice to both locks, then you can look to use the two together, engaging both your root and central lock along with the breathing. You most likely will have already been doing this to some degree, but now with a direct focus and a stronger force of will behind the action, you will find it to be a stronger practice. Remember though, there is no rush. Working with the locks can stir a lot of stagnant energy stored deep in the body and cause things to come to the surface that may be hard to face. There is no need to jump in at the deep end, take your time and slowly wade out from the shallows; especially if you do not know what is lurking in the deeper waters of your unconsciousness. It is easier to patiently journey forward than it is to recover from getting ahead of yourself.

As the throat lock is more mechanical, it does not need to be worked in such a way as the other two, but it is a good way to end any work you have done practicing with the Bandhas. If you find that the throat lock causes too much discomfort when breathing, then soften the strength with which you are holding it. It is possible that working the throat lock can cause coughing and other reactions that look to clear the throat, and provided it is not excessive or painful then this is healthy for your body and allowing a cleaning of this area that was previously inaccessible. If it does cause excessive reactions or pain, then look to work the lock to a point before this reaction occurs. I.e. if the full throat lock is 100% then find where on route is manageable for you to use. If 20% is where you can work, then that will be sufficient until such time in the future when you feel able to increase the degree to which you engage the lock.

Once you have reached a point in your practice where you are able to work with all three locks to a strong degree with no difficulties, then you may like to try Maha Bandha, "The Great Lock', comprising of all three locks used together. The great lock is an enormously powerful practice. This practice within yoga was only ever passed on from teacher to apprentice when the teacher felt they were at a stage where they were able to handle it, and so for generations it was kept quite exclusive amongst a small group of yoga masters. The great lock works with raising Kundalini energy in a powerful way, and so this really should only be attempted when a lot of work has been done with the bandhas on their own.

5 It's going to get emotional.

▨ LET'S GET FEELING.

I would like to share a meditation with you that is not so related to working with our emotions, but is to do with feeling. It is the meditation I found that allowed me to fully grasp what meditation was all about. When sitting comfortably and with your eyes closed, visualise yourself as a mountain. Feel your sturdiness, immovable and vast. Perfectly still and above is blue sky, all around you. You are timeless. Your roots hold you fast, whilst your head reaches high into the heavens. Above you are clear skies, and each thought you may find that passes by is a cloud. Clouds come and go; the breeze will bring them around you, though they pass on through the same way that they came. You can watch the clouds come and go without them ever changing what you are. There may be times when it seems like there is no blue sky to be found, maybe the clouds become a storm and you are surrounded by the dark, but you remain still and patient and safe in the knowledge that in time this too will pass. The clouds cannot adopt the qualities of the mountain, they can only ever be temporary to the permanence of the mountain. You can weather the storm, and when it clears, the blue sky is there once again.

What does it feel like to be you? This time we *are* talking about emotionally. If you were to draw a pie chart with each portion representing how you feel most of the time, which emotion would be the one you experience most? It may be a hard question to consider, especially if this means admitting to yourself that generally you aren't that happy but being honest with yourself is essential. Do not categorise each feeling but approach them with an equanimous mind. If we can see all our emotions from a balanced place of observation, then it gives us the chance to ask ourselves "What is this?" What does it mean to feel joy or anger? Why is it that what may frustrate you has no effect on someone else? What is the message connected to this feeling? Our emotions are complicated and often we may not even understand why we feel the way we do, but when we observe how we feel rather trying to ignore (attachment - aversion) it, we find ourselves with a powerful tool to navigate our lives. We find ourselves using our feeling mind, our intuition, rather than our thinking mind.

Depending on our line of inquiry, there are many systems where it is accepted that we have many minds. The idea of a "gut mind" is something recently being accepted in western science where it has become understood to be an important factor in the state of one's mental health. If we look at our mind as a centre for processing information, a place of input from the external, and output from the internal, then we can begin to understand the language with which each mind speaks to us and what each language feels like.

It is common to try to control our emotions by suppressing them. When we do not listen to how we feel for lack of understanding them and seeing them as something we would rather not experience, we give the way we are feeling the attachment of aversion. Suppression creates tension, and the tensions in the body causes it stress which leads to a reactive behaviour. Imagine a wild animal that has been wounded, and has been for a while, to the point it can continue it's life without much of an impact. You wish to help it, but as you go to touch the wound to clean it, the animal reacts and attacks you for being the cause of its pain. We as human animals are the same. When we find ourselves in similar situations of the past, we act in an aggressive and defensive way to protect ourselves, unaware that it is an old wound that needs to be dressed and healed.

To understand how we feel, we must first practice to feel. By now, having practiced a few forms of meditative techniques, you will have felt a few things that may range from enjoyable to unpleasant. We have begun to identify our attachments, what we are wishing to avoid and that which we wish more of. Whilst knowing what gives us a good feeling is useful in helping us feel better, to continue the journey into deeper truths that can be found in our practice we must not shy away from that which we do not enjoy. It is the unknown, the area outside of our comfort zone, that is the direction of our growth. Returning to an equanimous mind during these areas of our practice will lead to the release of the attachment, allowing us to listen from a place of understanding so that we may learn what we are telling ourselves.

As you work deeper inside of yourself through your practices, you may find emotions coming to the surface that do not seem to make sense. Allow this to be a part of the process and do not interrupt it, for this is the releasing of the stress caused by past suppressions. I have cried numerous times in meditations, and I have no doubt there will be many more ahead. Meditation is every feeling. Meditation is the giving up. It is the listening. The impatience. Frustration. Observe the process. It should not and could not be otherwise. Let go of the ideas of should and could so that you may be with what is.

To be aware of our emotions allows us to develop emotional maturity, a state of being that allows us a moment to decide how we act to our feelings, rather than reacting and flying off the handle, only being aware of how we have behaved after the damage has been done. Imagine yourself in a moment where a situation is approaching you; as you move toward it, it is moving toward you. The emotional impact of this situation is a ball of solid energy that is going to collide with you. To catch it face on will lead to you slowing down, sticking to you, a weight you carry around everywhere into the future, even though the moment belongs to the past. To ignore its impact completely may lead to its impact being greater than you can handle, and so it knocks you over and leaves you out of balance, less prepared for what comes next as you get back to your feet. We must learn to dance with each moment and the energy that it brings to us, stepping through each situation prepared to hold whatever comes our way, able to absorb and move with the force of the impact it has on us, using its momentum to keep us moving forward as we turn and spin, dancing with each moment in our hands, and letting go when it no longer serves us. Life is a dance of holding on and letting go, so we should look to embody and express Anicca (Impermanence) in every step.

No doubt there has been a time when another driver has performed poorly that led to you reacting as they cut you off. Something beyond your control has forced you to react for safety which stirs some primal emotion in you and you now feel anger at this other driver for their decisions. How quickly are you able to let go of this feeling? This other driver is now speeding off far away from you and is totally unaware of you or your emotions. Yet the feeling they stirred inside of you: you still carry with you. In that time, you are distracted, and for all you know you may be doing to another what one has just done to you. Your focus is with something that is now elsewhere, your attention is to the past and you are not fully aware of your current surroundings, leading you to impact another driver, who could impact another, and so on. Can you forgive this other driver? Ok, they were a threat to your safety in that moment, but what if you learnt that this driver was rushing to a dying loved one? It is possible, or perhaps in that moment they had simply not calculated very well and would be apologetic if they knew. Are you able to claim that you always make the best choice in every situation? Whatever the reasoning for their actions may be, it is irrelevant, all that is required from you is to let go and be aware of the moment you are in now. You are responsible for your own peace.

There is a framework for recognising and understanding our minds, a system known as Chakras. Chakras are the points in the body where our Nadis (the channels of prana) intersect, where Yin and Yang meet. These energetic centres can be imagined as a spherical Yin and Yang, the two energies coiling through and around each other like a snake. Each Chakra is connected to a focus of the mind and relates to an area of your physical body that holds the space responsible for the energy behind your feeling. This idea is already subtly in the way we speak when we use phrases such as "butterflies in your stomach", "frog in the throat" or "big/open hearted". We understand, in some way, that areas of our bodies are related to emotion, even if we are not fully aware. Using the Chakras helps us to understand this on a deeper level.

As our Nadis thread throughout the body, there are many places of intersections and so with this we have thousands of chakras, thousands of points throughout the body where Yin and Yang come together. You are a constellation of points of energies, like the stars above. Depending on the system of belief you work with there can be any number of "main" Chakras, but it is generally widely recognised that there are 7, and as an introduction to Chakras it will be easier to start off small until the idea is better understood.

The 7 Chakras are as follows:

Chakra	Location of the body	Colour / Visualisation
Sahasrara	Crown, top of the head	Gold
Ajna	Third eye, mind's eye, centre of the forehead	Deep dark blue/ Almost black
Vishuddhi	Throat	Blue
Anahata	Heart centre, breast area	Green
Manipura	Solarplexus, just beneath the rib cage	Yellow
Svadisthana	Lower abdomen, just below the belly button	Orange
Muladhara	Base of the spine, genitals	Red

Each Chakra comes with its own characteristics, relating to an element such as fire or water, that can be harnessed when one is balanced. Without care of these energies, it is possible that these energy centres are out of balance with either the Yin or Yang more dominant, or with a blockage causing a lack of any energy. For example, Manipura is seen as the centre of our confidence, and when one is nervous or worried one may experience the sensation of "butterflies in the stomach." It is this physical part of ourselves that is where our emotional energy gets trapped, so we are unable to digest and assimilate this feeling, which in some cases can lead to vomiting. Manipura is represented by the element of fire, our digestive fire, and a fire without much energy is a weak one, leading to low confidence and poor digestion, so these would be signs of a weak/deficient Manipura Chakra. It is also possible to have excessive characteristics of the Manipura where one would act with an over-confidence, having too much fire they could act aggressive and dominating. We will come back to the qualities of the Chakras but let us first practice on them where we only need to be aware of their locations.

Using the practice of Ajna centring pranayama, we can use our counting of the breath to bring our focus to the area of where Ajna Chakra is. To start this practice, bring yourself to a comfortable sitting position, and closing your eyes, begin with Sama Vritti Pranayama to come into your breathing and your body. After some time of sitting practicing Sama

Vritti Pranayama, the equal ratio breathing, we then change the ratio from 4:4:4:4 to a count of 8:4:8:4, making the inhale and exhale twice as long as the suspension. Remember to make this manageable, it does not need to be forced or strained, breathing in this fashion however works for you provided the ratio is the same. So if need be, you could breathe to a count of 4:2:4:2, or if you are counting fast or feel you could breathe further then a ratio of 16:8:16:8. As you practice with each breath, observe where your internal focus travels.

After some time with your Ajna practice, you can finish your sitting with Anahata centring pranayama, to spend some time in your heart space. The breathing ratio for this is 7:1:7:1. Again, be sure to make it comfortable and feel the internal movement this creates. Inhaling for a count of 7, holding the inhale for a count of 1, exhaling for a count of 7 and holding the exhale for a count of 1. As you control your breath, observe where your focus gathers inside of your body and be aware of this space of yourself with the energy that it holds. After a few rounds of this practice, then stop controlling your breathing, dropping the counting of the breath and allow yourself to breathe naturally, keeping your attention to your breath until you are ready to come out of the practice.

Whenever we practice a meditation or breathwork, always try to blend the start and end of your practice. Do not see it as a start and stop, as black and white, but more as a gradient as you ease into your practice, gently entering your meditation. It is the same to come out, do not just suddenly stop and jump up out of what you were doing, but transition gently, as if you are extracting something delicate from the process and you wish to carry it with you without disturbing it. It is a continuous process, a steady incline without any steps.

Maybe this breathing has not yet connected you to any area of your body and so you feel you are none the wiser on where these Chakras may be located. This is natural, it certainly took me a while before I felt there was anything to these pranayamas, or even the Chakras. In my own journey, the framework of Chakras was too far into the realms of spiritual practice and were too abstract for me, so I completely rejected the system, focusing my efforts on that which I found to be more substantial instead. But in time, after enough practicing, eventually it led me to connecting my experiences with this framework of understanding. I had received a chart on Chakras in my training and had put it to one side with no intention of coming back to it. But one day, as I sifted through pages of information and notations, I came across this chart and it had a loud message for me. The chart was like the previous one, but it also had details on the traits of Chakras, like this:

Chakra	Function / Quality (Balanced)	Excessive Traits	Deficient Traits
Sahasrara	Awareness, Connection	Overly intellectual, A sense of elitism, Spiritual addiction, Confusion, disassociated body	Fatigue, Learning difficulties, Spiritual scepticism, Limited beliefs, Apathy
Ajna	Intuition, Imagination, Purpose	Anxiety, Headaches, Nightmares, Delusions, Difficulty concentrating	Insomnia, Lack of Clarity, Poor memory, Poor vision, Denial,
Vishuddhi	Communication, Creativity	Excessive talking, Arrogance, Inability to listen, Stuttering	Colds, Fear of speaking, Weak voice, Poor Rhythm, Lack of creativity
Anahata	Love	Co-dependency, Poor boundaries, Possessive, Jealous, Love-addict	Lack of Identity, Shy, Lonely, Isolated, Lack of empathy, Bitter
Manipura	Power, Will	Dominating, Stubbornness, Blaming, Aggressive, Bossy, Manipulative	Eating disorders, Weak willed, Poor self-esteem, Passive, Low confidence
Svadisthana	Pleasure, Sexuality	Overly emotional, Substance abuse, Poor boundaries, Sex addiction, Obsessive attachments	Not in tune to own feelings, Stuck in a mood/ feeling Frigidity, Impotence, emotionally numb, Fear of pleasure

Muladhara	Survival, Stability	Negativity, Greed, Heaviness, Sluggish, Monotony, Hoarding, Materialistic	Fear, Constant survival mode, Lack of discipline, Restless, Underweight, Spacey

This chart is in no way exhaustive, and do not take it as gospel, as with whichever lineage or system you follow there will be some variations, but you get an idea of the framework and how the Chakras correspond to how you feel and the character traits they influence.

Energy in all forms is constantly fluctuating, so if you find yourself in one of these boxes, do not see where you are as a place of permanence. Remember, it is a spectrum, a gradient that you can transition along. We all have the same capacity to behave in some fashion, and we all share the same capacity to change the ways in which we behave. All it takes is an awareness, some time, and the ability to forgive yourself when you stumble along the way. To choose to be a certain way is a constant process, but the longer you establish a pattern of behaviour then the easier it will be as it grows into a new habit.

When this chart first resonated with me, I saw the excessive traits of the Sahasrara Chakra and instantly recognised myself as a spiritual addict. On my road to recovery, I shifted from being addicted to chemically altering my physiology to spiritual practices and a "spiritual lifestyle." With all my energy in this area I was disassociated from my body in a way that had made me stiff and robotic. It showed me that I needed to work on moving my energy into other areas of my life, to those things that brought me pleasure, grounding me and allowing me to loosen up. To have fun with life.

Once you have familiarised yourself with the breathing techniques and found your awareness to settle on the areas of Ajna and Anahata Chakras, it would be a good experience to return to your bandha practice, but now rather than just observing the physical practice with the body, observe the energies that you find in the locks. The Mula Bandha (root lock) works with the space that is connected to the Muladhara Chakra, Uddiyana Bandha (central lock) to Svadisthana and Manipura, with Jalandhara Bandha (throat lock) being connected to the Vishuddhi Chakra. With these locks and centering breaths, you now have the tools to bring awareness into areas of your body and your energy. Strengthen your connection to these areas of yourself and notice if anything stirs when you rest your attention in the spaces inside of you where your Chakras can be found. To feel nothing is to feel nothingness, and this is an indication of little to no connection. To feel resistance or discomfort is to find stagnant or dense energy that rests in that area of you. Whatever it is that you find, remain the observer with an equanimous mind and have faith in the intelligence of your body that it can respond accordingly. Your body knows how to take care of itself.

Another practice, but this is a quick one. Just as you are right now, close your eyes and bring something to your mind that makes you smile. Some amusing memory or a good joke. Maybe that cat meme you saw on the internet the other day. As soon as the thought is present, notice what happens to your body. Recognise how the thought arrives, and there is an instantaneous reaction from the body in feeling and display of emotion. It is this quick and easy to affect your mood. This practice would work for any other emotion you choose to dwell on, though for now that is not something we need to explore. When how we feel is so instantly affected by what we are thinking on, it pays to be aware of what we are thinking about.

Your mood can affect your thinking, but your thinking can affect your mood. To be aware and have the ability to recognise where your thoughts or mood are, will provide the space to take a moment of self-reflection and allow you to navigate forwards in the direction of your choice. The key is to remember that you are not your thoughts or feelings, you are that which hears and sees them. You are not your thoughts or feelings, no more than you are your finger or foot. These things are a part of you, not you yourself. If you were to lose your finger or foot, you would still be you, so do not fear losing a thought or feeling. You are the omnipresent awareness that observes these ever-changing phenomena. To identify with these tools would be like an explorer claiming they are their compass, who would spend the rest of their lives moving in whichever direct[...] compass needle turns, forgetting that it is they who cho[...] where to go, not the compass.

To become aware of how we are feeling requires us to become more sensitive to our emotions. This can seem a choice that most would rather avoid, for why would anyone choose to feel emotions such as sorrow, any deeper than they already do? To hide from the pain of sorrow means that you will never be able to heal the damage. This is what creates the suffering of pain, to be attached in aversion to that which is an intrinsic and essential part of life. Scans of people's brainwaves have shown that the brain behaves in a similar way when physical and emotional pain is experienced. Both forms of pain are as real to us as the other, because when you are in it and you feel it, you know it is there. However, we can understand physical pain easily when we can see the damage it has done to our body, so we do not dwell on it. We know that the body will heal and repair itself. But when we experience emotional pain, we cannot always see where the pain is coming from, and it can seem as though the whole-body hurts, that you are nothing but pain. With our aversion to this, we try to hide from what we feel and in doing so ignore the truth we so desperately need. Dive into the depths of what you are feeling and when you are surrounded by the darkness, all you can do is give in and accept the pain is real. In that moment, take the time to understand why you feel this way and you will know why you o longer running from the truth, you recognise 'our pain and at the same time you see which ight is. Maybe you have lost someone, or you thing. Without it, you feel its loss. How lucky you nate to have lived with something so precious and dear to you that to be without it brings you such pain. To see the beauty in the truth of your sorrow allows you to smile with tears and provides us the gratitude to have been blessed enough to be provided something so essential to living. To open up to the feeling may provide a deeper sorrow, but it permits us a greater joy too. It is the largest trees that receive the most light, that must also grow the deepest roots into the darkest places. Yin and Yang.

The experience of an equanimous mind, a life free from attachments, means that we will be liberated from our suffering. But we will still experience pain, for pain is essential and cannot be avoided in life. We must remember that to feel pain is not suffering. To feel pain is to be alive. It is to hold on to pain that will create our suffering. To feel the pain of sorrow is natural, but to hold on to this feeling, being attached in aversion, leads one to being depressed. Understanding our pain allows us to accept it as our current experience, and the knowing of Anicca reminds us that eventually it will pass. However, living without attachment does not mean detaching ourselves from life. Detaching yourself would be to not hear how you feel and would have you walking through life as a robot, simply functioning and existing rather than living and thriving. We can also view our emotions as a spectrum:

$$\text{Sorrow} < - - - - < - - - - < 0 > - - - - > - - - - > \text{Joy}$$

When we view this concept in a linear format, it would seem that we could only feel one thing at a time. Yet it is possible to find we experience many emotions simultaneously. In our most joyful of moments, we can remember that this moment is passing, and in doing so, find the sorrow in joy. In our most sorrowful moments, we can see the beauty of such a feeling and be joyful to have had something so special. Rather than seeing the equanimous mind, that 0 point, as the space in the middle of the spectrum, see it as the circumference that surrounds the spectrum, our awareness behind our attachments. The equanimous mind can watch all that we feel without being disturbed, much as the way that a strong wind can create a choppy sea, but the deep ocean remains unaffected in its stillness. The surface can weather all seasons, the deep watches.

Meditation can consist of focusing on a single element of the self, or it can use many. The following meditation, known as the Blue Mist Meditation, requires the synchronising of our focus on breathing, visualising, and remembering. Due to the multiple elements of this practice, it is not an easy one to get the hang of, especially if you are not a naturally visual person. It is important to remember that you are practicing however you can, not how you think you should be. Whether your practice is as you had imagined or not, it is working for you as it can right now.

Begin by adopting your meditative position. Start to tune in to yourself, checking in with yourself physically. Checking in with yourself mentally. Checking in to your energy. Find your immediate experience and let all else fade away. Allow yourself to be here in the now. Centre your attention on your breathing and feel the flow of the breath moving in and out. Observe the rhythm of your natural breath. Follow your breathing until you feel ready to guide your breath deeper. Breathing in through your nose, feel your belly expanding, your rib cage lifting, breathing into the crown of your head. Exhaling, falling with the breath, contracting as the breath leaves you, helping your diaphragm, using your abdominals, pulling the belly button to the spine. Continue. Every inhale, fuller than the last, looking to breathe beyond your maximum lung capacity. Every exhale, more complete until lungs are empty, ready for the next breath in.

Find yourself breathing with your whole body, no longer just the belly or lungs, but the whole of you in a constant flow of toing and froing, breath coming and going. Feel your breathing moving through every pore of your skin. Every breath in, breathing through each pore, every breath out, breathing back out through your skin. Full body breathing. The whole body expanding and contracting.

Continue breathing like this as you return your focus internally. With awareness resting here, stir memories of your day. Bring memories of the week or month. Bring to you whatever memories that come naturally. Be in their energy, how they make you feel and hold that energy inside of you. Take your time, see what rises and what you have been holding on to. There may only be one or there may be many. Whatever comes is what you carry, but now see what you hold inside of you. Continue. Keep them coming.

When you are full, when inside of you swirls with as much as you can gather, breathe deeply into all of them. Fill each memory and feeling with your breathing, digging deep with every inhale, pushing out with every exhale. As you breathe out through your body, see everything that is inside of you now coming out, through your skin, as a blue mist. Every breath in, grab a hold of all that is inside of you. Every breath out, take the energy from inside to the outside with the breath. Slowly. Slowly around you this blue mist grows thicker, as what was inside now comes through, outside of you. Continue, bring out all that there is until you are surrounded by a mist so thick that you cannot see through it. Sit in this cloud of blue, still in the swirling energy around you.

Freeze it. Freeze the mist so now you are within solid ice. A deep glacial blue surrounding you. That which was inside of you, is now outside of you, frozen all around. As you sit in stillness, look out at the past, of memories and feelings you once held. In the centre, in this place of equanimity, see all these experiences as parts of the journey that have brought you here. Neither good nor bad, just life unfolding as it does. You are no longer who you were when these things happened, see with eyes of understanding and know it was all meant for you so that you could Become. Spend time here, look at it all. When you are ready, bring your awareness back inside, back into you, into your heart.

Centred in your heart space, feel the warmth of your heart. Visualise a flame here, the source of your warmth and light, the energy that you release into the world. As you breathe, feel this warmth growing, the flame inside of you expanding and emitting light from you, and with it the heat of your heart. As you radiate your warmth, the ice around you begins to melt. Above you, as the ice thins, you see this present moment. All around you, this moment right now will be all there is. The ice melts and trickles away until you emerge from it, into all that there ever really is. Now. Be Here Now. All that once was, is gone. These things you held on to, are gone. Feel how this present moment holds you so lightly, with nothing weighing you down. You are so warm, your light is so bright, your heart is open and all who feel it, can see it. Spend time here.

When you are ready, breathe deeply, getting ready to bring your practice to a close. There is no rush. In your own time, transition from your practice and when it feels right, open your eyes.

If you found that there were elements of this meditation that you could not connect with, recognise what you were unable to manage. Observing the areas of your practices where you feel you do not connect with allows you to check whether you are not connecting, or whether you are imagining that it should be different to how it is. For example, those of us who did not manage to connect to the visualisation of this practice, what does it mean to you to visualise? This was something I always struggled with. I imagined that to visualise would be like seeing with your eyes closed much in the same way as with your eyes open. But this was not the case. I started to say, "I cannot visualise" and "I guess I am just not a visual person". I had put a block on this element of my practice and so whenever any visualisation work was presented, I would just return to my breathing or physical experience.

Eventually, I met someone who said, "Picture your front door". In that moment, I understood. I can see my front door and describe it perfectly, just not in the way I had imagined I would. So, should you find yourself unable to bring a vivid blue into your visualising, draw from what you know; the ocean, the sky, the blueberries you had in your breakfast. Whatever you can connect with, allow that to support the areas of your practices that you feel a lack of connection to. Until the moment of clarity, the intention is enough. It simply takes some time and patience.

6 No time for your mind games.

▓▓ LET'S GET THOUGHTFUL.

After my initial training and studies, I no longer wanted to become a teacher. I had begun my training believing that was what I was meant to do, but when it came time to advertise myself as one, I dragged my feet. For a long time. Eventually, (I cannot remember why I did, but I did) I found a room and managed to round up a bunch of people to pay me to share with them how to meditate. Before every class there would be a swirl of emotions inside of me, my instincts telling me to turn around and run away, save myself from what must surely be judgement and failure! But it was too late, I had to, and I pushed past this reaction to do what I said I would do.

I was aware this was happening inside of me, though I did not pause at any moment to ask why. With each course that I taught, this reaction would present itself, but it would lessen each time, until eventually, it was no more. What was it that I was afraid of?

What was happening to me each time I moved past the fear? Death. I was afraid of dying. Not physically dying, but the form of my identity and who I believed myself to be. Up until that first class, I had always been the student, never the teacher. I had stepped from being the one who did not know, to the one who did. This paradigm I had grown up with my entire life was now being reversed. My own initial experience of school was one where to be the smart kid led to being bullied, and years later through the teenage years of school, to be the one to put up your hand and answer the questions was not seen as being very cool. Teachers were these tyrants who, if they were not droning on about some subject, they were disciplining you for misbehaving. They were boring, and more often than not, old. My experience of school had led to a definition of what a teacher was and this idea was deeply rooted in my subconscious, for it was not something that I would have to think about, it was just what I knew to be true. I knew myself to not be that, to identify as something other than what a teacher was. This was my obstacle; the changing of who I was.

Who we think we are is a character we dress ourselves as, so that we may interact with the world around us. It is a necessary tool to navigate our lives so that we may relate to our environment and other people. It allows us to think of ourselves in relation to something else, creating a sense of individuality. To be free from ego removes the separation to the external world so we become like the rain drop in an ocean, immersed in the oneness of all things. As pleasant as this may seem, to have no sense of self would have you doing nothing, for there would be no one to do anything for. We must wake up each day and dress ourselves in the characters we choose to play. Remember when you were a child? You could change freely from fairy to firefighter in one day. When did you stop dressing up? Why?

You already have multiple characters that you perform as, whether you are aware of it or not. For example, the version of you with your mates on a Friday night, is that the same version of you that interacts with your boss at work? Or the you that attends a music festival, are they the same as the one who attends a funeral? We constantly adapt and shapeshift the way we interact with our environment and situation, yet who we are beneath the outfits remains the same. The problems arise when we attach ourselves to our identity, believing that we are the character we dress up as.

Imagine what it would be like if a Shakespearean actor stepped off stage without breaking character and walked to the local bank to discuss a mortgage in old English. Everyone would be able to see the actor was clearly performing, they would see through the illusion and not take them seriously. The actor would not be able to connect and communicate with those around them, instead isolating themselves in a world of their own imaginings. There is a time and place to be on stage, and another for sitting amongst the crowds.

It is commonly misunderstood in the spiritual world that we are looking to attain an ego-less state on a permanent basis. For those that fall for this ideology, they will either find themselves with the biggest unchecked ego or become forgotten to the world. Acting as if we do not have an ego can only be an act of suppression; denying the existence of something does not mean that it does not exist. To believe that one does not have any ego is to ignore a necessary tool for coexisting within a community, unless one can truly live in a state of no ego, in which case the one would see no need for the community just as the community would see no need for them. Children have fun in playing out their charactered roles amongst each other; we must remember that we are those same children, too. Instead, to find that state of ego-lessness is a goal to be discovered in our meditation practice so that we may remember every garment we dress in. It is the core skill necessary to put yourself in "another's shoes."

How does this benefit anyone? I will share with you an example from my own life. My family life became unhealthy and a lot of hurt and pain was spread between my father, my mother, and my sister. As the son and brother, my relationship to my family became one of anger and resentment which would cause me to act out in a way that only exacerbated the pain between us. The identity we share amongst our families is the deepest-rooted of the ideas of who we believe we are. If who you are with your friends is your t-shirt and trousers, then who you are with your family is the underwear beneath, making it the hardest to be aware of. The underwear that I wore had become soiled, and no matter how I dressed myself over it, I would always feel the discomfort. To throw this shit back at my family only led to more being spread around and there seemed to be no point in the future where it would ever get any better - until I found a state free from being a son and brother. Through my practice, I found myself as that which wore the fabrics of my identity, and in doing so was able to strip myself bare. This allowed me to recognise that my pain was not my own, that my family members held their own too, with some suffering much greater than my own. It was in that place that I could find compassion for the ones I blamed for the pain I felt. It was stepping beyond the paradigm of the familial relationships that I could see each of us for all we are, little children stumbling through a complicated and strange world. My father was no longer my father, my mother was no longer my mother and my sister no longer my sister. We were just kids in our pants who needed our bums wiped. We all are. We must first wipe our own bums, stick our clothes in the wash and take care of ourselves before we can help others to do the same.

A tool is neither good nor bad, it all depends on how that tool is used. Nothing that we inherently have is a problem, unless we believe it to be one. The same tools we have created to help us build can also be used to destroy, the only thing that can change the outcome is the user of the tools. A hammer can be used to build shelving, or it can be used to smash that same shelf to pieces. The tool that is our thinking mind is designed to be a problem solver, it enables us to look at problems and questions to discover the answers. Therefore, if we use our thinking mind on all things, then all things are problems that require solving. How much energy is spent trying to fix something that is not broken?

The ego hates change, because to become someone else requires that who we are now, dies. We are never more ourselves than when we are around others, each other's ideas of who we are keeping the other in check. Who we are in relation to one another, always having an audience to perform to, will make sure we are never able to remove the outfit we find some comforting. An affliction of ego is to hate being alone, to find it uncomfortable or unbearable are signs of an individual who lives with an unchecked ego. Simply being alone can show these persons many things, and meditation when alone will provide the space to observe where the inner turmoil is stemming from. We must discover what remains when "I" no longer exists.

The ego fears death, but if we do not allow ourselves to die then how can we become reborn? How can the timid become confident? The quiet become loud? The weak become strong? With impermanence being the absolute truth of the universe, to hold on to old constructs of who we think we are will see us falling behind. Does the tree fear its leaves will never grow back? Does the rose panic that its petals will never bloom again? To grow and die, to grow again, is the rhythm of nature, new life growing over the old. Learn to shed your leaves and dress yourself in different ways, adapting to your environment as it changes around you. Grow in the direction that you choose, focusing growth on the areas of who you are that you wish to nourish and that feels to be the greatest and truest version of who you are. Not all blossoms will grow to bear fruit, so keep focused on what you do have, not on what you lack. At school I was a sapling, and the version of me as a yoga teacher is the tree. I wanted to branch out but feared the weight of growing would be too heavy to handle, for I had forgotten to recognise my own growth since I first sprouted.

A healthy and recognised ego is a tree that moves with the breeze, flowing with the current of its surroundings. An unhealthy and unrecognised ego is a brick wall, a barrier to the outside, protecting that which is inside. Each brick of this wall is an attachment to a belief that was laid down by a younger version of you, one that did not know as much as this version of you now, one that did not know any better. With walls around us, we can only look upon what is outside with judgement, for anything outside of these walls is "wrong" or "dangerous". We cannot smash down the walls around us for they were securely built over a long time, our conscious thinking patterns moving to the subconscious to become a deep habitual pattern, a modality of functioning that we act from. Each brick must be carefully removed, slowly erased from our psyche, allowing us to move into the grounds of understanding. Your walls may turn out to be bigger or smaller than you had first imagined, but patience in practice will remove all obstacles. You may feel one day that your walls are gone, only to encounter a new situation that triggers a behaviour in you that you had not recognised before, and you will see there is more work to do. There will always be more work to do. We did not just build these walls ourselves, but together, over generations. There will be bricks your parents handed to you. Others, that their parents handed to them. How far back do you carry the weight of your ancestors? Is there a part of you that functions in a state of survival from when life was once a battle to exist? You may find there are not just walls around you, but the platform from where you stand is a foundation built by us too. Where will you find yourself when you no longer have anywhere to stand? What if gravity is a brick?

What if time is too? Our addiction to time has led to an affliction where we are all in such a rush; impatience saturates society. We are doing to have done, so that we may do the next thing. Speaking to have said. Listening to reply. Eating to have eaten. Fucking to have fucked. We have all become tangled up in this belief to the point that the present moment is the least recognised. Where are you if not here now? There is such a franticness to be doing something, making the most of our time and being productive, that the symptom of boredom is the most common affliction that we all regularly suffer from. So focused on time, we assign everything we do with a level of preference, and in doing so become addicted to what we prefer, craving more of the same and avoiding that which we do not. Meditation is the biggest threat to time, and its hold over us will be the first to present itself for the majority. As a wild horse must be broken before it can be ridden, we must hold on to our practice, no matter how hard our Sankaras look to throw us off. Keep holding on and eventually you will find mastery over the wildest of beasts.

Deep habitual patterns are caused by a conditioning of our minds. The conscious repetition of an idea leads to the idea being believed without needing to think on it, much like how one learns to ride a bike or drive a car. The repetition of a thought is called "Mantra". There is a form of meditation commonly known as "Transcendental Meditation" which involves the use of Mantra. Mantra translates to "Mind liberation" but also "sacred message / charm / spell". A mantra is a word or a phrase that you repeat to yourself over and over again, in a way like the counting of the breath in your mind, but now with the power of language and meaning. You will have been using mantras your whole life, but without being fully aware of the thoughts you have been repeating. It could be anything, "I am ugly" / "I am depressed" / "I don't deserve this", repeated daily, maybe even multiple times a day until you believe it to the point you no longer repeat it. Now that idea weighs heavy in you and you no longer need think it because it is just something you now "know".

A mantra must be an important message, but it cannot be a lie. If you are sitting to meditate with mantra and repeat to yourself "I am happy" when in fact you are very upset, it will only lead to a denial of feeling and interrupt the communication between you and your body. Remember, denial is suppression which creates tension. Denial will only mask the truth and keep you from being in the equanimous mind of understanding. It would seem to make sense that to change something such as what we think or feel about ourselves, we would enforce the opposite idea, and potentially this may lead to the outcome we aim for, but the process of letting go completely provides freedom from that form of thinking in its entirety. To chase happiness, we will always measure it with sadness, they cannot exist without each other for they share the spectrum of emotion, this is the nature of duality. Rather than subscribe to the spectrum, with an equanimous mind we can transcend this ideology, for the words are spells cast long ago that mould our beliefs. To fully understand what they aim to explain, we must first step outside of them. The words we use are a circle drawn around the essence of what we are trying to explain, so we must not look at the container but the space inside of it. Look here long enough until the shape is lost, and the essence is understood. You will know you have found understanding when you are able to capture this essence in a shape of your own.

I found using a phrase to which I did not know its meaning which provided me with a sound I could connect my own definition to. The phrase I used was "Om Namoh Shivaya." When I first read this all I knew was that it was of Hindu origin and that was enough for me, I did not wish to find out anything more, because I had already given it my own meaning. In this phrase I put that which I was looking for, it held for me the essence of what I was looking to find with my practice every time I sat down to meditate. It would be hard for me to put into words what this phrase meant to me, it was closer to being a feeling than an idea. The repetition of this mantra during practice, and even throughout the day, allowed me to remember the space that I could create by checking in inside of me. It was a rope from the heavens that allowed me to climb out my thoughts and with a higher perspective, see what was going on.

As this was my experience with mantra, I cannot imagine using a phrase in my own tongue, so I would suggest that a mantra needs to be like a catchy part of a foreign song that you do not know the meaning of, so you can provide it your own meaning. Then again, if there is one that works for you, go ahead! Here is a few if you are not sure where to look:

Om/Ohm/Aum --- Om Namoh Shivaya --- Om Mani Padme Hum ---
Ho'oponopono --- Dainichi Nyorai

There are hundreds of mantras to choose from and they can be found amongst the many sects of all spiritualities, but all you need to do is find the one that sounds right to you. To practice with a mantra in meditation, all you need to do is repeat the phrase either out loud or internally. It helps to find a rhythm with the phrase that you use, and then as much as possible, always use this rhythm with your mantra. You can do this however you like, though it does help to connect the mantra to your breathing. For example, if you are using the Om Namoh Shivaya mantra, then as you inhale you can say "Om Namoh" and as you exhale say "Shivaya". The wonderful thing about mantra is how easily it can be utilised wherever you are, in whatever you are doing. For instance, if you are in your car encountering another questionable decision by someone else on the road and you check in to notice you are still chewing on your tongue about the incident, you can let go of the mental chatter and engage the use of your mantra. However, it should not be used to ignore that which you think about. It is not a sound to be shouted louder than the others, do not look to talk over yourself. Always look for a smooth transition from your thoughts to your mantra, rather than reacting. We must still recognise what our thoughts dwell on so we may accept that part of ourselves.

Exploring mantra can unveil many things about ourselves due to the mechanism of how it works, as the mental repetition of an idea can shape our perspectives, becoming the foundation from where we stand and look out into the world. If I were to ask you to say to yourself something like "I am beautiful / I am good / I am worth it" repeatedly, would you believe it? Maybe, maybe not. There will be many of these ideas that we struggle to believe about ourselves, especially when we apply it to different areas of our lives. Maybe you feel you are beautiful on the outside, but not on the inside? Or vice versa? Each belief you "know" about yourself is a brick you have built into a wall around you, the walls that make up our ego.

A wall is built to separate one thing from another, a defence of the thing that is inside from the outside. Our ego is also a tool that looks to save us from that which we have learnt to hurt us. But an unchecked ego builds walls so high and so wide that we wall ourselves in, unable to move in a world that is forever moving. You cannot always be as you are now. Think of you at the age of 2 and 7 and 11. 13, 18, 25? Who you are has changed more times than you may know, the shape of who you are shifts through the unfolding of your life, and maybe some walls have fallen away through the ages, but there will be many walls that remain standing. One stands behind their wall, looking out at the world beyond, and with judgement defend themselves as to why they will not join those beyond the wall. "Oh no I don't dance" / "I can't do that, I just can't" / "No I don't like those kinds of people". We impose limitations on ourselves for fear of what that means to our identity.

Some of us refuse to dance for fear of what others will think of us. When examined, the truth is closer to the fact that we fear our own judgements, and often, it is we who are the ones judging others. Others who are not worried about what you think of how they look and are just having fun. Some of us will never attempt to try something because we do not think we are capable of it, when the truth is closer to the fact that we fear failing or making a fool of ourselves. Some of us will judge a group of people due to certain traits they share, deciding that they are lesser to ourselves because of how they look or act, when the truth is closer to the fact that we are the lesser ones for subscribing to a mindset where we feel so inferior that we must elevate ourselves above others to feel better about ourselves. The walls and the reasonings are endless, the complexities of the experiences one goes through in life and the thoughts and ideas that churn inside of us are so uniquely created that our egos are ours and can only ever truly be understood by our Self. It is only when we start to question the beliefs that we hold that we can start to tug at the threads that make the safety blanket we wrap around ourselves. From inside the blanket, we think we are safely behind a wall, a fortress, when from the outside it is seen as a thin veil that some can see straight through. We must step outside this illusion we disguise ourselves with and start questioning why we are the way we are.

As we permit ourselves to open to this dialogue between ourselves (the ego) and our Self (that which wears the ego), we can start to hold down each thread we find and keep tugging until we trace it back to its first stitch. Say you are 30 now, and you hate fish. You have always hated fish and you have hated it for so long you haven't eaten any for about 15 years. That idea, that belief, was first sewn when you were 15 years old, and for 15 years you have had such an attachment to that disgust you felt when you tasted fish, you have not dared to try any ever since. Now, after your friend has talked about how delicious this fish was on several occasions, you start to think maybe you will try it yourself. After all, that is not the fish you had before, it is a different fish and cooked in a different way. With courage, you pick up some of its meat on your fork and as you bring it your mouth you are ready to react in revulsion, that old habit is still there even as you take the food from the fork and have that first bite...and then you realise, "Oh, that's quite nice actually!" You may not always like the next fish you try, but at least you are exploring new possibilities beyond what you once believed to be true. Do not let an old version of yourself rule who you are now.

The recognition of ego can be an uncomfortable process, at times even painful. But how can this illusory mental construction cause us to experience physical sensations? The relationship between the mind and body is a psychosomatic one. The definition of psychosomatic is "Relating to interaction between mind and body. / (A physical illness or condition) caused or aggravated by a mental factor." In this way, the entire body is a reflection and expression of the mind. In Buddhism, these deep habitual patterns are referred to as Sankhara. These Sankharas, the information of our subconscious programming, is stored in our bodies as tension that starts to bleed out the longer we go against its functioning. For example, you may by now have started to recognise similar sensations stirring up each time you sit to practice your meditation with the most common Sankhara we all encounter on this journey - the feeling of boredom. Have you ever thought about what boredom is? It is a feeling we often experience, but it is not an emotion. The affliction of boredom is an attachment to the idea that there is something else preferable than your immediate experience, an attachment to the idea that at some point in time, in the future, there will be something better to experience. Boredom is a distraction caused by the absence of presence in this moment. At the root of boredom is the attachment to time and a mentality of lack. There is a fear that our time is limited, that we do not have enough of it, and so must spend as much time as possible doing nothing except that which we want to do; we cannot waste any of our time. So, what can we do when we sit, and the discomfort of boredom distracts us from our practice? We must carry on, with an equanimous mind, observing our experience without reacting. The struggle is in realising that to overcome these hurdles, they require us to do nothing about them at all, for it is the sitting through every sensation without feeding it that allows the Sankhara to be released.

When you initially sit down to practice, you make yourself comfortable. You adopt the sitting position that works best for you, and then you are still. Slowly, the longer you sit, discomfort starts to become more apparent. Yet when you first sat, these feelings were not there? And were you to react to these feelings, to get up from your sitting position, these discomforts quickly dissipate. Where did they come from? And where did they go? The information stored in our bodies is a tension, a reactive process of defence to bypass the thinking mind. The feelings that present themselves whilst you sit are much like being given a massage. You are pressing on an area of tension that will feel uncomfortable until the tension is gone, and the muscles relax. Not all knots can be teased out in one sitting, it takes regular attention to remove the tighter ones, but with patience the body can let go and you find yourself loose and free. If a flowing river encounters a large stone in its stream, the river will continue but energy will be taken from the flow and over time sediment will deposit around the obstruction. The energy of our body is the same, where these knots interrupt the flow of our prana and cause a build-up of dense energy that sits and stagnates. Just as the rock in the river is slowly being eroded by the water, the tensions and dense energies in our bodies are released as we allow the body to be still, giving it time to work on that which is otherwise worked around.

Often, if not all, Sankharas are born through pain, and the fear of being hurt again. We find ourselves in a situation that we suffer and wish to never experience again, so a reactive behaviour is installed so that we may protect ourselves from it. This has its purpose, for if we could not learn to retract our hand from the fire then we would not last long. Physical damage is an easy issue to navigate, but emotional damage can be hiding around the corner, or often hiding in plain sight. Pain is essential, and we can never avoid it, but suffering pain is a choice. To fear pain and wish to hide from it, to live in aversion and live without understanding, this is the cause for the suffering of pain, for in the attachment we carry the pain with us, always, never letting it heal.

Each point of suffering is a rope that we bind around ourselves, restricting ourselves from living freely. As we go through life, we wear our bondage so well that we assume this is how it is supposed to be. I have uncovered many bindings in my meditations, so many Sankharas weighing heavy on me. For example, I was at a 10-day Vipassana meditation retreat which consisted of a total of 10 hours meditation a day, where for the whole time you are there, you do not talk, read, write, or communicate with anyone in any form, avoiding eye contact at all times. You are completely in yourself. Yet as I walked around between sittings, I found myself asking "Why are they annoyed at me?" or "Why do they have a problem with me?" regarding anyone that passed me by. These passers-by gave me no attention in any form, yet I was feeling as though they had an issue with me. I would think "Did I break my silence?" or "Did I make a noise in the meditation hall?" and so many other thoughts to try and figure out why it was that I had upset my fellow meditators. Until the truth hit me. They did not even know I was there. They were paying me no attention at all. I was projecting aggression onto those around me and reacting defensively, guarding myself from them. I discovered that this was how I interacted with people I didn't know, I would have this defensiveness that would gradually dissipate over getting to know the individual, but until such time I would treat those who I did not know as threats. Recognising this part of me that I had not seen for so many years was enough to allow me to release the behavioural pattern, and since then I engage with those I meet in an open and friendly manner. This behaviour could have been picked up from being bullied at school, or some other time in my life, it is impossible to fully know where the Sankhara came from, though it does not matter. What does matter is recognising who you are right now and deciding whether this is the way you wish to be or not.

I will share with you one more unbinding from my journey. It was at another meditation retreat where I had been meditating through pains in my body, looking for an equanimous mind whilst the psychosomatic sensations intensified and faded away. I had sat through much by this point in my journey, until I came to one that was in my right knee. It was an intense pain, and a black hole to my awareness, sucking all my attention into it so every time I meditated all I could do was focus on the pain. Many meditations were spent with frustration and impatience rising, feeding the pain, at points making the pain spread from my knee to my whole leg, making it feel like it was swelling and twisting. At one point, I internally screamed "DO IT" ready for my leg to be broken if that was what it took to break the Sankhara. But all that did was feed the pain and the binding was wound tighter. Eventually, I managed to find equanimity in my mind and spend long enough there that the pain could bleed out, until eventually it left me altogether. Even though I was sat in the upright meditation position, with all my concentration, it felt like my forehead was on my knee, but as the pain released, my attention slowly started shifting up from my knee, through my body. It was floating up my body, and as it started to go through my head, I felt like I was about to have an out of body experience. To remain calm and breathing was the focus so as not to become excited at what was about to happen. I reached the crown of my head, and I opened my eyes. I pulled back from the experience because a sudden train of thought steamrolled through my mind, "What if you shit yourself?" It was a fair point, for if I were to leave my body then surely, I would no longer have control over its function? Suddenly, I would have soiled myself amongst 200 people and how would I have ever dealt with that situation! It made sense, though disappointing, the trade-off was not worth the experience. Even if I were to only break wind amongst 200 silent dedicated meditators, as I had heard many others do, that is not something that I would allow! It wasn't until a year or two after this whilst participating in an active guided meditation, where we were directed to "remember our inner child", that I was transported back to when I had been about seven years old on a family dog walk. I had been walking with my family and godparents in the Lake District where we had gone to their friend's house to say hello. I needed the toilet but chose to wait until we got back to the house we were staying at. The walk was longer than I could manage so the inevitable happened, and I ended up walking a long way, very ashamed of myself and very uncomfortable. I had been carrying that emotional memory for almost 20 years without realising. It had been there hiding and influencing many choices and decisions, but it seemed so sensible and rational that I had never stopped to think that it needn't be such a concern. As an adult (with a fully functioning sphincter) it doesn't need to be a concern at all.

A realisation is not always enough. Realising that you act a certain way because of choices or actions that you made does not always result in you changing that behaviour in yourself instantly, but it can provide the want to change that behaviour. We might recognise something in ourselves and believe the work is done and we will no longer continue to behave the same way, and although this may be the case in some areas of your life, the root of this behaviour will still be there. The behaviours we exhibit and may recognise in ourselves are like the leaves of a tree, for there will be many situations where the same issue expresses itself in different ways. We must remain constantly aware of ourselves so that we work to pluck the budding leaves before they grow, giving us the ability to start chopping away at a modality that has grown over time, until eventually the roots are no longer fed and they die off, giving us freedom from the worries of the past.

I was misled for a long time in my practice as I was caught up on an idea of a word that had been used when studying the levels of practice in meditation. I had been told that there is a "layer of bliss" to be found, and so in my early practice I couldn't help but keep searching for this "bliss". Every time I sat to meditate, I would end up finishing thinking "Well where the hell is it?" I was so set on finding what I thought bliss may be, that I was missing the whole point. You cannot see what is going on around you if you are looking somewhere else. It wasn't until another guide came along and used the words "point of experience" that I realised where my attention should be. I found that bliss was not somewhere deeper along in my practice, but in the immediate present moment of my experience. It is so easy to get caught up on the words that one uses that we forget to hear what they are actually trying to say. Words are used to convey a message or a meaning, but vocabularies are so varied from person to person, especially when it comes to dialects or different languages, that it is easy for the message to be lost in translation. Kind of like when two people look at a painted canvas and one may walk away wondering why the artist is considered an artist at all, whilst the other walks away with a deep understanding of the artist's meaning. The former was too caught up on the literal image on the canvas whereas the other was seeing the message that the artist was looking to express. When it comes to spiritual practice, it is easy to be put off by the language used. Whether the language seems esoteric or belonging to some ancient dialect, this may move one to take their attention somewhere else, and if you find this happens in your journey then look to swap out the words that do not connect to you for something else. For example, I have used the words awareness or energy, which could hold the same meaning as the word spirit does to a practitioner of another system. Our words are our thoughts, and our thoughts are abstractions from our experiences, so to find understanding we must first consider the abstraction of the essence being presented to us, not the packaging that it comes in.

Everyone you meet is a mirror that will permit you to see into more of who you are. It is what my thanks at the beginning of this book means, "To those of you I have already met, thank you, for teaching me so much. If I am yet to meet you, thank you, for what you will teach me." They will show you parts of yourself that you would otherwise hide from yourself, for it is these shadowy spaces that do not fit in with the idea you have of who you are. When you find that another's impatience disturbs your peace, it is because you do not recognise your own impatience. Perhaps the display of impatience before you is unnecessary, perhaps it is unjustified, but when you suffer your own impatience, does it come from the present situation that you are being in, or has it been a string of events throughout the day? Maybe even a string of events throughout your life that has led to your disposition. Displays of emotions overwhelming someone are often triggered by a single moment, but it is that moment that has tipped the scales, like a single grain of rice. We cannot see the troubles that have led to the emotional reaction from someone else, and most of the time we cannot see it in ourselves either. But it can be found through each other. This is where the skill of present awareness learnt from meditation must be brought through each waking moment, so that we can fully observe what is happening to others, as well as to ourselves. It is when encountering disruptions and disturbances between ourselves and others that we can recognise something about who we are. When the emotions of others no longer pull us in, when we hold our own space whilst others are stumbling with theirs, we will have found our emotional maturity, allowing us to remain in our peace.

There are difficulties in this work. When you take a step back and see yourself from a different perspective and speak to yourself honestly about who you are, to recognise your ego and actively work on changing who you are. Looking at yourself and recognising your own limitations, accepting that you are responsible for your own failings is challenging, but also the people around you can make this a difficult process too. When we meet people, a paradigm is quickly established of the "relationship to other", where who you are is enforced by those around you. With these people you will always be expected to perform as the same character, and anything outside of this will create a discomfort. The catch with being more aware of yourself is that you become more aware of others, and the games we play with each other come to light. Those of us who are manipulative or dishonest become easy to spot, and you may realise people you have kept in your life for a long time do not permit you to be the person that you would wish to be. The people you love may also be those who hold you back. This can be a hard pill to swallow. It can bring on anger and resentment, leading to an action that comes from reaction, which can only lead to a further unhealthy situation. If something must be done, it must be done with the anger, for this is the force pushing you to change. But we must use the anger mindfully, not reactively, otherwise this only leads to more work. It is possible to be angry at someone with love, like when a child is about to run into a road when they know they should not. In this way, when we become angry with those we love, we must not hide it. We must witness the movement inside ourselves, and only when the anger is understood can it be discussed in a healthy manner. In these discussions, the sensitivity of the words we use are heightened as emotions are exposed at the surface and so truth must be expressed without hatred or malicious intent. The issue must never be made out to be anyone's fault, for the fault is shared by all involved. Accepting responsibility in every situation allows you to change the dynamics between yourself and others, so that moving forward you do not replicate a similar exchange. It is the ego that wants to make the Self right and the Other wrong, but this dynamic is not balanced for it is performed by an aggressor. This will only lead to further problems to untangle, with the Other either being a victim or an aggressor. Ask yourself, is this my ego talking? Are these words spoken with equilibrium?

7 This is unknowable.

◼ LET IT BE.

In the deepest parts of all that we are, all we have is what we believe. What we believe in shapes our perspective of our experiences in life, and with this they can be the hardest to recognise and work with; the bricks beneath our feet. Much like the story of the princess and the pea, the sensitivity required to feel these things under layers upon layers of all else that we are can only come with a regular, committed, and patient practice.

To worry about anything is like anticipating the approach of a dark fog, fearful of what it may contain - the unknown - and panicking that when it arrives, the worst will happen. You close your eyes and brace for impact...but it never comes. You open your eyes and realise you have already been swallowed by the darkness, and though you may not be able to see far, you realise this fog has no substance and cannot bring you harm. Be patient and find your centre, hold your focus and soon enough the fog passes on.

Curiosity killed the cat. From its ashes out climbed a lion. Do not allow fear to contain your curiosity. Every fear we step beyond will lead to our death, but each death will become a rebirth. Each rebirth, an evolution. Growth is the process of constantly evolving, and in a world that is constantly growing, there will always be new directions to grow. Which directions we grow in, will be our choice.

Picture a spider's thread hanging from a tree. So slight and delicate, the softest of disturbances to the air will cause this thread to be moved. The experience of stillness is just as slight, just as delicate. With an underdeveloped force of discipline, the slightest disturbance can keep us from the feeling of suspension that this stillness has to offer. When we come to our practice, initially it may seem impossible that this stillness is even there to begin with. You will sit and sit until...wait...was that it? A glimpse. For a moment, though you may not be entirely sure, you might have just found it. Keep going and the glimpses become a seeing, until the seeing becomes a knowing, and eventually when the knowing is understood, it is a being. With this stillness inside, it doesn't matter if a thunderstorm is throwing the spiders web around for it was never about the direction the thread was hanging in; the stillness is in the thread itself.

In an ever-changing world, there is no such thing as a constant. Impermanence (Anicca) is the only consistent thing. Every platform of belief is a rule we impose on an unruly world, and when the rules are broken, we don't like it. We point at water flowing through a channel dug out in land and call it a river, but no sooner has the word passed our lips then it has already moved on and what we called a river has gone. How dare this experience of mine be anything other than what I demand it to be! The mistake we make is believing it to be "mine", as if the experience **belongs** to us. We then label and categorise the world around us in the same way we identify ourselves, and by this feeds us the illusion of control. To "know" something is to attach ourselves to an idea that requires us to no longer give the known thing much attention anymore. It is only when our "knowing" is challenged that we see the attachment we hold. The challenge stirs our defensiveness as we wish to protect what we identify as being right from the alternative wrong.

The experience does not belong to us. We belong to the experience. The identification and therefore the attachment with the experience of life, making it something personally owned, is the cause of this pain. This is our experience, a collective experience, and it cannot conform to everyone's rule. How could it? When one says, "all must be up!" and another says, "all must be down!" how would this turn out? You would not be able to go anywhere at all. Add more individuals with their own directions to the mix and it would have you inside out and upside down. Instead, we must recognise the interpretation of the experience from each unique perspective, understanding that over many lifetimes, shared down through the blood, are infinite thoughts and ideas that manifested into the individual before you.

How can we explore the rigidity of our beliefs that shape our perception? Your perception is the glasses through which you see the world, and each belief is a layer of glass that creates the lenses. It is impossible to take the glasses off to begin with, we need them to see, so we must clean them where they sit. You begin your work and notice some dirt and scuffs on the top of your lenses, so you immediately get to work to clean this up. It may take some time, but eventually all the dirt and scuffs are gone. You know what to look for now, your ability to focus grows stronger, and gradually you see dirt and scuffs on the lens closer to the eye. You clean. And so, it continues, layer by layer. Until one day you are ready to let go of seeing the world through anything but open eyes that now know how to see all things clearly.

Depending on how deeply entrenched the idea is in you, the degree of difficulty in letting go of it can be hard to determine. The trains of thought that we have are just the ones we can see coming into the station, but the routes that these trains come from have a vast network leading back to an underground that exists deep within your subconscious. Imagine stations all at the end of their lines, with networks branching off with more stations as you go further into the heart of the land, and if you traced all these networks back to the centre you would see they all originate from the same place of birth – Fear - The fear of dying; Ultimate death and other deaths along the way, such as that of the identity, the ego. If this ultimate truth cannot be accepted, if you always hold on to the idea of death as an aversion, fear will always manifest in your life. When we die, we realise the worries that we hold on to, those that we cling to life for. There are easy things, like loved ones, it is good to recognise who it is that we care for, but there are things we cling to that can make death feel like hell. Guilt. Anger. Fear. When you are slipping into a place beyond time, dragging these sufferings with us can last for an eternity. These feelings can be such a core element to who we are as a character. We let them kill us a little bit every day. When you see that person and it stirs anxiousness or a lurch of guilt, without the conscious recognition and work on this part of ourselves, it will continue to exist, feeding on the energy we give to it when we react to our triggers. The handling of our triggers has led to this word having a bad connotation. When we imagine triggers, we imagine the things we wish to avoid at all costs for the feeling they give us is something we wish to hide from.

Every thought is a single thread of a spider's web. If you follow a thought back to where it came from, you can find all the intersections and points of your life that the belief system has influenced and manifested. We know the closer we get to the origin of all these thoughts, the closer we get to facing the spider that created them. We imagine this spider to be grotesque, terrifying and life threatening and so we do whatever we can to avoid looking into its many eyes. But with courage, you realise it is not as you had imagined it to be. Possibly initially there is disgust or revulsion, but understand that the spider exists, just as you do, and it was a younger, less aware version of you that mistook the spider for a beast when in fact it is totally unthreatening.

It is healthy to approach all practice with scepticism rather than to believe in the truth of another which will only ever have you as a follower. Practice until you believe in your own experience, until you understand in your own language, for this is what spirituality is about. Do not be led by belief in another, be your own leader and walk the route yourself. You must come into your own power.

So, importantly, don't believe in a single word that I have said.

8 Love

■ IT IS ALL THERE REALLY IS

The first 9 months of our existence are provided with everything we could ever need. We are fed, warm and cared for. Within our mothers we are kept safe, and all we find as we prepare to come into this life is that we are loved. We may have no memory of this time, but it is imprinted on us from the time we came from not being, into being. When we join this world, we are mostly provided with all that we need. But gradually, the provisions from those who care for us becomes our own responsibility, and how we are weaned from this state into being the provider for ourselves can influence how we seek out these necessities. For a child to suddenly be left alone without an answer to its cries, they may grow to crave the comfort of another's company, seeking out the figure that abandoned them, or they may become a person who only understands solitude, shutting others out. The removal of an expression of love can leave a void that can either never seem be filled or hurts to go near. It is these empty spaces we must learn to fill from the inside, to give ourselves what we need so that we do not depend on it from another. This is what it means to come into our own power. To be all that we need to be, giving us the freedom from unhealthy coping mechanisms, we must become a complete person from the inside before we can have a healthy relationship with anything in the outside world.

To take this journey of self-exploration will always lead to an inevitable outcome - compassion. To discover yourself and recognise all the sufferings that you are responsible for, will lead to you having compassion for yourself whenever you slip up or act out in a reactive manner. This compassion will not only be to yourself, but to everyone you meet, as you start to see how you have not been alone in the struggles of suffering. To recognise the sufferings you have carried will lead you to recognising the sufferings of others, as recognising our behaviours related to what we feel devoid of will also help us observe what others feel devoid of as well. It is when we lack compassion for what another has done that we are presented the opportunity to recognise something about ourselves that we have not yet understood.

There is a practice to add to the end of any meditation called Metta, which translates to "loving-kindness". After your meditation, spare a few minutes to send out into the world the energy you have cultivated in your practice. Ensure it is a good energy, one of love and compassion, and send it to those closest to you. Send it with the intention that they

*will benefit from your meditation practice just as much as
you. Over time, as you practice this sharing of energy, you
can start to send it out into the wider world, to those that
may not be as close. Even to those you may consider the
"enemy." When you come to the end of your meditation,
spend a moment longer focused on love. Connect to your
love for yourself. The love you have for others. That others
have for you. That we share for each other. That all of life
is founded on.*

Throughout the lives of many, love has been shared over and
over again. All that love, every kind of love, has led to the
creation of you. You are an embodiment of love, the ultimate
expression of it. No matter the hardships and struggles of life, it
is beautiful, nonetheless. Love is why you are alive.

Picture the biggest tree you have ever seen, with leaves beyond
count. It is stood by the bend in a river, its roots reaching down
into the passing water, its branches hanging overhead. Every
leaf of this tree is an ancestor. Every branch is their lives, their
stories, all running into each other, leading to the story that
we all share. The trunk is the flow of life, always and inevitably
moving toward you. Toward Now. You are the point where
the water and root meet. All the roots are the lives that you
are connected to, each seeking and moving through the
dark to keep it all going, to sustain the tree of history, of your
ancestors, of our ancestors, reaching back to the seed from
which all life grew, reaching into the ever flowing current of

possibilities waiting to become the rest of your life - life around you, life beyond you. Do not get swept up with the speed of life around you, stay moving in the unique direction of your growth. Honour those that came before you by making the most of all that you can be.

Make your life worth all the suffering that it has taken to bring you here, beginning with freeing yourself from your own suffering. When we free ourselves, we live by an example of how others may do the same.

I Love You.
Max.

Printed in Great Britain
by Amazon

56028407R00066